DATA A

BCS, THE CHARTERED INSTITUTE FOR IT

BCS, The Chartered Institute for IT, is committed to making IT good for society. We use the power of our network to bring about positive, tangible change. We champion the global IT profession and the interests of individuals, engaged in that profession, for the benefit of all.

Exchanging IT expertise and knowledge
The Institute fosters links between experts from industry, academia and business to promote new thinking, education and knowledge sharing.

Supporting practitioners
Through continuing professional development and a series of respected IT qualifications, the Institute seeks to promote professional practice tuned to the demands of business. It provides practical support and information services to its members and volunteer communities around the world.

Setting standards and frameworks
The Institute collaborates with government, industry and relevant bodies to establish good working practices, codes of conduct, skills frameworks and common standards. It also offers a range of consultancy services to employers to help them adopt best practice.

Become a member
Over 70,000 people including students, teachers, professionals and practitioners enjoy the benefits of BCS membership. These include access to an international community, invitations to a roster of local and national events, career development tools and a quarterly thought-leadership magazine. Visit www.bcs.org/membership to find out more.

Further Information
BCS, The Chartered Institute for IT,
First Floor, Block D,
North Star House, North Star Avenue,
Swindon, SN2 1FA, United Kingdom.
T +44 (0) 1793 417 424
F +44 (0) 1793 417 444
(Monday to Friday, 09:00 to 17:00 UK time)
www.bcs.org/contact
http://shop.bcs.org/

DATA ANALYST
Careers in data analysis

Rune Rasmussen, Harish Gulati, Charles Joseph, Clare Stanier and Obi Umegbolu

© 2019 BCS Learning & Development Ltd

The right of Rune Rasmussen, Harish Gulati, Charles Joseph, Clare Stanier and Obi Umegbolu to be identified as authors of this work has been asserted by them in accordance with sections 77 and 78 of the Copyright, Designs and Patents Act 1988.

All rights reserved. Apart from any fair dealing for the purposes of research or private study, or criticism or review, as permitted by the Copyright Designs and Patents Act 1988, no part of this publication may be reproduced, stored or transmitted in any form or by any means, except with the prior permission in writing of the publisher, or in the case of reprographic reproduction, in accordance with the terms of the licences issued by the Copyright Licensing Agency. Enquiries for permission to reproduce material outside those terms should be directed to the publisher.

All trade marks, registered names etc. acknowledged in this publication are the property of their respective owners. BCS and the BCS logo are the registered trade marks of the British Computer Society charity number 292786 (BCS).

Published by BCS Learning and Development Ltd, a wholly owned subsidiary of BCS, The Chartered Institute for IT, First Floor, Block D, North Star House, North Star Avenue, Swindon, SN2 1FA, UK.
www.bcs.org

PDF ISBN: 978-1-780174-33-4
ePUB ISBN: 978-1-780174-34-1
Kindle ISBN: 978-1-780174-35-8
Paperback ISBN: 978-1-780174-32-7

British Cataloguing in Publication Data.
A CIP catalogue record for this book is available at the British Library.

Disclaimer:
The views expressed in this book are of the authors and do not necessarily reflect the views of the Institute or BCS Learning and Development Ltd except where explicitly stated as such. Although every care has been taken by the authors and BCS Learning and Development Ltd in the preparation of the publication, no warranty is given by the authors or BCS Learning and Development Ltd as publisher as to the accuracy or completeness of the information contained within it and neither the authors nor BCS Learning and Development Ltd shall be responsible or liable for any loss or damage whatsoever arising by virtue of such information or any instructions or advice contained within this publication or by any of the aforementioned.

Publisher's acknowledgements
Publisher: Ian Borthwick
Commissioning Editor: Rebecca Youé
Production Manager: Florence Leroy
Project Manager: Sunrise Setting Ltd
Copy-editor: Mary Hobbins
Proofreader: Barbara Eastman
Indexer: Matthew Gale
Cover design: Alex Wright
Cover image: andreiuc88
Typeset by Lapiz Digital Services, Chennai, India.
Printed by Hobbs the Printers Ltd

CONTENTS

	List of figures and tables	vii
	Authors	viii
	Foreword	x
	Acknowledgements	xi
	Abbreviations	xii
1.	**INTRODUCTION TO DATA ANALYSIS**	**1**
	What is data analysis?	2
	Advances in computer science	6
	Advances in data storage	7
	Advances in data processing	9
	Advances in statistical and machine learning	10
	Legal and ethical considerations for data analysis	12
	How the IT industry can address the challenges of data analysis	16
	Summary	20
2.	**THE ROLE OF DATA ANALYST**	**22**
	What is a data analyst?	22
	Affiliated roles and differences	23
	Key industries where data analysts work	24
	Nature of tasks undertaken by data analysts	26
	Data analyst key responsibilities	29
	Data analyst key skills	30
	Summary	49
3.	**TOOLS, METHODS AND TECHNIQUES**	**50**
	Tools	50
	Methods	56

	Techniques	69
	Summary	88
4.	**RELEVANT REGULATIONS AND BEST PRACTICES FOR DATA ANALYSTS**	**89**
	Working with other people's data	89
	The regulatory response	91
	General Data Protection Regulation (GDPR)	92
	Data security	102
	Data governance	109
	Data quality	111
	Engaging with the organisation – the data community	120
	Data provenance	124
	Summary	127
5.	**CAREER PROGRESSION OPPORTUNITIES**	**128**
	The changing role of the data analyst	129
	Career opportunities	129
	Building a career as a data analyst: getting started	135
	Building a career as a data analyst: developing your role	141
	Career progression: what next as a data analyst?	147
	Career planning	148
	Summary	157
6.	**A DAY IN THE LIFE OF A DATA ANALYST**	**158**
	A typical day in the life of a data analyst	159
	Top tips for data analysts	173
	References	176
	Further reading	178
	Index	180

LIST OF FIGURES AND TABLES

Figure 1.1	Data analysis disciplines	5
Figure 2.1	Key data-related roles and differences	23
Figure 2.2	Skills needed as a data analyst	25
Figure 2.3	Typical product life cycle	27
Figure 2.4	Key tasks and soft skills required	33
Figure 3.1	Simple graph data model	53
Figure 3.2	Examples of correlations in different data sets	64
Figure 3.3	Example of interpolation and extrapolation	67
Figure 3.4	Examples of imperative and declarative code	71
Figure 3.5	Example ER diagram showing a simplified student enrolment system	80
Figure 3.6	Example of a star schema	83
Figure 4.1	A simple data lineage map	126
Figure 5.1	SWOT analysis	157
Table 4.1	Suggested approaches for data quality dimensions	117
Table 5.1	What qualifications do you have or are about to achieve?	149
Table 5.2	What experience do you have that might be relevant to a data analyst career?	150
Table 5.3	What technical skills do you have that might be relevant to the data analyst role?	151
Table 5.4	What personal skills and abilities do you have?	152

AUTHORS

Rune Rasmussen is an independent analytics consultant with more than 15 years' experience of implementing risk management and monitoring projects in the financial services industry. He holds a BSc degree in computing, a BA degree in mathematics/statistics and a MSc degree in computing with a focus on computational support in the statistical R package for Big Data analysis. He is a member of BCS, The Chartered Institute for IT and a fellow of the Royal Statistical Society. He has worked with several large companies within the insurance, banking and investment sectors on projects to improve risk analysis governance, and regulatory and financial data analysis. Rune is the author of Chapters 1 and 3.

Harish Gulati is an analyst and modeller based in London. He has 15 years of financial consulting and project management experience across leading banks, management consultancies and media hubs. He is passionate about demystifying his complex field of work. This has led him to be a speaker at analytical forums. He has also authored the book *SAS in Finance* (2018) in which business cases are analysed using various statistical models. He is a trustee with Third Age Project, a charity working with the marginalised elderly in the UK. He has an MBA in brand communications and a degree in psychology and statistics. Harish is the author of Chapter 2.

Charles Joseph has been working in the areas of data governance and quality for 15 years, across professional services, insurance and retail organisations. He established Datazed Ltd in 2017 to provide consultancy services, demonstrating how good data management can support increased revenue, decreased costs and reduced risks. He was particularly keen to contribute to this book in recognition that there is an ever-increasing requirement for people who are trained to understand data, its uses and how to analyse it so that assessments can be made and questions answered.

Charles has a BSc in mathematics from Imperial College London and is a chartered fellow of the Chartered Institute for Securities and Investment. Originally from Liverpool, he now lives in London with his wife Lisa and four sons. Charles is the author of Chapter 4.

Clare Stanier is a senior lecturer in information systems at Staffordshire University. She has a PhD in computing (information systems) and she is a member of BCS, The Chartered Institute for IT and a senior fellow of the Higher Education Academy. She teaches, researches and publishes in the fields of data management and artificial intelligence. She is currently working on a number of research projects on digital innovation, Big Data applications and machine learning for small and medium enterprises (SMEs). Before joining Staffordshire University, Clare worked for a number of different organisations, including the NHS and a national charity. Clare is the author of Chapter 5.

Obi Umegbolu is actively engaged with BCS, The Chartered Institute for IT as a data analyst subject matter expert in designing the UK government's Data Analyst Apprenticeship Programme. His tasks with BCS include syllabus and examination bank development multiple choice questions (MCQs), as well as the Synoptic Project creation. Obi is currently a data analyst skills development coach in the emerging technology areas of Big Data and data science. He has been an advisor to several organisations looking to develop academic programmes related to data analytics and project management. Prior to his current role, Obi held senior analytical roles in data quality projects in public- and private-sector organisations in the UK and Africa. He is a certified PRINCE2 Project Management Practitioner and earned a BEng and MSc in engineering from University of Portsmouth, UK. Obi is the author of Chapter 6.

FOREWORD

If data is the new oil or soil or whatever the latest description is, then this book is the receptacle to collect that oil, observe it and then pour it somewhere useful and get great value from it.

I just wish when I stumbled into my data career, from my original golden choice of an actuarial career, I could have had a comprehensive view of what I was letting myself in for. After all, data is a journey not a destination!

Who knew that massively open online courses (MOOCs) would become a thing and actually could be vital for your progression in the data and analytics profession? You will read all about it in Chapter 5 of this book.

The world needs data analysts, to work with business people to better define problems and to deliver insight – not just a bunch of spreadsheets with no explanation. Whilst I have often thought we analysts were numbers people, this book has made me realise we also need to be words people too.

Perhaps you've completed a bit of data analysis at university but almost certainly with a small, clean data set with no outliers and a receptive audience ready for your nuggets of insight. Well, make sure you read to the end of Chapter 6 and you'll realise what life as a data analyst is really like. Not the bed of roses you may have thought, but trust me it will be rewarding.

Graeme McDermott,
Chief Data Officer, Addison Lee

ACKNOWLEDGEMENTS

Thanks to Catherine, my wife, and to Freya and Lena, my daughters, for their continued support and encouragement during the time it took to develop this book.
(Rune Rasmussen)

This has been possible due to my wife and son's endearing support and for letting me off those precious family moments. Thanks Kalindini and Parth.
(Harish Gulati)

Thanks to Lisa, my wife, for her ongoing and unceasing support. To our boys – Aron, Micha, Eitan and Yishai – I hope that you will also go forward and share what you have learned with others.
(Charles Joseph)

Special thanks to Paul Shufflebotham, MBCS, for allowing us to draw on his experience of working as a data analyst.
(Clare Stanier)

My sincere thanks to Chinwe, my wife and Kamsy my son, for their support and understanding throughout the period of writing this book.
(Obi Umegbolu)

ABBREVIATIONS

BAU	business as usual – is the continuous process of working towards a business goal, as opposed to an improvement project that will create a step change
BCS	BCS, The Chartered Institute for IT – formerly known as the British Computing Society
BI	business intelligence is a company function that produces data about business operations
CDO	Chief Data Officer – a senior managerial role that is tasked with looking after the company's data
CPD	continuous professional development – an official requirement of many professional bodies for their members to document continuous individual development of skills and competencies
CPU	central processing unit – the main processing hardware in typical computers
DPA	Data Protection Act – a law in the United Kingdom designed to protect personal data in electronic or paper form
ER	entity-relationship – a type of modelling usually associated with relational databases which focus on the connections (relationships) between things or concepts (entities)

ABBREVIATIONS

ETL	extract, transform and load – a sequence of data manipulation activities normally associated with data warehousing
GDPR	General Data Protection Regulation – a regulation in European Union law that protects the privacy and data of all residents of the union
GPU	graphical processing unit – a processing unit specifically built to deal with graphical data, but increasingly used for advanced data processing
HNC	Higher National Certificate – a UK further educational qualification that covers the equivalent of 1 years full time study
HND	Higher National Diploma – a UK further educational qualification that covers the equivalent of 2 years full time study
ICO	Information Commissioner's Office – an official independent regulatory body in the United Kingdom that has been tasked by Parliament with ensuring the protection and privacy of personal data
IDE	integrated development environment – an application that offers facilities to make software development easier, such as a code editor with syntax checking, and assistance with debugging
IoT	Internet of Things – internet connected network of physical devices, interacting, collecting and sharing data, which can be remotely monitored and controlled
IP	Internet Protoco – an IP address is a numerical identity assigned to every device connected to a computer network
JSON	JavaScript Object Notation – an open-standard file format that uses human-readable text

ABBREVIATIONS

KPI	key performance indicator – measures put in place to assess job performance
MI	management information – data extracted and summarised to assist management in making better strategic decisions
MOOC	massive open online courses which are provided on the internet to non-collocated students who learn and interact exclusively with electronic tools
NoSQL	non SQL or not only SQL – a set of tools and techniques for dealing with information that is not suitable for traditional relational databases
NVQ	National Vocational Qualification – a UK qualification that assesses candidates' knowledge and skills
ODBC	Open Database Connectivity – a programming interface for connecting relational database systems with other systems and languages
OLAP	online analytical processing – a tool used to perform multidimensional analyses of data
ONS	Office for National Statistics – the independent body in the UK that publishes official statistics
PAF	postcode address file – a lookup file from Royal Mail that contains all delivery addresses in the United Kingdom
PCI DSS	the Payment Card Industry Data Security Standard – an industry standard that covers information security for credit cards
PECR	The Privacy and Electronic Communications (EC Directive) Regulations 2003 – a UK law implementing EU regulations and gives individuals specific privacy rights
PII	personally identifiable information – data items that could be used to identify an individual

PRINCE2	Projects IN Controlled Environments – a structured project management method
RDBMS	relational database management system – a software system designed to manage storage, access and processing of data so that it can be accessed according to the relational model
SDE	software development environment – programming tools with features to assist in writing code
SFIA	Skills Framework for the Information Age – a framework for skills and development of IT professionals that is promoted by BCS
SLA	service level agreement – an agreement between a service provider and a customer that defines the level of service, such as the time it should take to complete a task
SME	subject matter expert – a person that is generally considered or officially nominated to be the expert in a specific area of knowledge
SQL	Structured Query Language – a programming language for extracting and processing information from relational databases
SWOT	strengths, weaknesses, opportunities and threats – a technique used to identify relevant factors that can help a company or an individual to achieve their objectives
UML	Unified Modelling Language – a standard for modelling and describing software systems, components and behaviour
XML	Extensible Markup Language – a markup language that defines rules for encoding documents in a format that is both human- and machine-readable

1 INTRODUCTION TO DATA ANALYSIS

This chapter aims to give a general overview of the current state of affairs in the data analysis discipline. Some of the areas covered in this chapter will be dealt with in greater detail in later chapters of this book.

> Unleashing the value of data is still at the heart of many organizations' strategy, and data analysts and scientists are becoming crucial in creating an innovative, digital and customer-centric organisation.
> (Patrick Maeder, Partner, PwC)

We begin with a description of data analysis and comment on the growing role that data has in our society. Then we introduce the technical advances relating to data analysis that have been made in computer science, data storage, data processing and statistical/machine learning during the last decade. These are the building blocks of the technical tools that enable the processing and analysis of 'Big Data'.

There are an increasing number of regulatory and legal requirements about how to deal with data, with very severe penalties for non-compliance. The subsection 'Legal and ethical considerations' in this chapter will introduce this area.

The chapter ends with a section on what the IT industry is doing to address some of the challenges that relate to the data analysis discipline.

WHAT IS DATA?

The existence of data and information predates our computers and the internet. In fact, data has existed in many forms, such as oral stories, wooden carvings, paintings, written records, storybooks, newspapers and so on, for thousands of years. However, this book is only concerned with data that is stored in electronic formats and can be processed by computers.

The Merriam-Webster dictionary defines data as 'factual information (such as measurements or statistics) used as a basis for reasoning, discussion, or calculation'.[1] Wikipedia defines data as 'the values of subjects with ... qualitative or quantitative variables'.[2]

Both of these definitions capture important aspects of data that is used for analysis. It is interesting that the Wikipedia definition draws attention to the difference between qualitative and quantitative data. Quantitative values are numerical and categorical, such as that typically found in a table or list, and they have been used for statistical analysis for many decades. Qualitative values are usually text descriptions, such as documents, emails or social media posts, and are rapidly gaining in importance for data analysis.

WHAT IS DATA ANALYSIS?

Wikipedia's definition of data analysis is particularly relevant to this book: 'a process of inspecting, cleansing, transforming, and modelling data with the goal of discovering useful information, suggesting conclusions, and supporting decision-making'.[3]

---

[1] See www.merriam-webster.com/dictionary/data

[2] See https://en.wikipedia.org/wiki/Data

[3] See https://en.wikipedia.org/wiki/Data_analysis

It draws attention to the fact that the process of analysing data includes the tasks of manipulating the data by cleaning and transforming it as well as the task of discovering useful information from it. Manipulating data is typically classed as a computer science skill, whereas the discovery of information from data is a statistical or machine learning skill. Successful data analysis requires both of these skill sets.

There are a number of standard process models for data analysis, most notably CRISP-DM, SEMMA and KDD.[4]

The role of data in society

Data analysis is rapidly becoming one of the most important and challenging activities to drive the improvement of business performance, public services and other important aspects of society. This is happening because the volumes of data we have available for analysis continues to expand, the technological hardware that is accessible to us grows in data processing power and the algorithms that we can apply to the data become more and more advanced. These factors mean that we can get better insight from data than ever before.

This insight is used by businesses to develop products and services that more precisely suit their customers and increase business profits. These developments in data analysis also benefit other areas, such as the public sector, where the data is used to find the most cost-effective solutions to benefit all social groups.

There are continual new announcements in the press, commercial trade magazines and academic literature of novel applications of algorithms, automated decision-making and more efficient strategic decisions based on data. These news stories remind us how important data analysis is in transforming political debate, the provision of public services, commercial performances and solving research questions.

---

[4] You can see a comparison of these models in this paper by Ana Azevedo and M.F. Santos: https://recipp.ipp.pt/bitstream/10400.22/136/3/KDD-CRISP-SEMMA.pdf

But these achievements are only possible because there are skilled data analysts able to work with the technology, apply the algorithms, explain the analysis and communicate the results to decision-makers. The growing importance of data in decision-making is creating an increasing demand for the education of new data analysts and the advancement of skills of experienced data analysts. To be successful and to keep up with all these developing areas, data analysts need a combination of skills that enable them to extract, process and manipulate data using programming languages and databases as well as statistical skills and acumen in communication. The role of data analyst is detailed further in Chapter 2.

Management expectations of data

So much of modern society is being transformed by a changing attitude to the role of data and the insight that we can get from its analysis. This change comes from growing expectations that decision-makers in these areas have of the importance of a scientific approach to data analysis and in the increasing use of automated decision-making.

Managers and administrators expect data analysts to calculate accurately and report on past performance data in their areas in addition to making projections and predictions of what the future will hold for their business. This isn't new.

In the past, the collection of data was somewhat expensive, and it was often collected for only one purpose. Now, leaders of businesses and public services are realising that the price of collecting data has become much cheaper and there is much more of it available in their organisations. The falling price of data collection also means that it is easier for organisations to procure data (ethically) from external vendors and there is a growing amount of free public data available for use, such as the British government's data.gov.uk initiative.[5]

---

5 See https://data.gov.uk/

Business leaders are now increasingly demanding that data analysts make use of all this data to help answer business questions to a greater extent than ever before.

Cross-disciplinary cooperation

Data analysis is a broad discipline and analysts cannot be experts in all the specialist skills required, so it's often necessary to draw on the competencies of other professionals such as database specialists, statisticians, machine learning experts, business analysts and project managers (see Figure 1.1). These professions need to work effectively alongside data analysts, appreciate the challenges faced and understand the results good data analysis can produce. Data analysts should ensure that they have at least a basic understanding of these disciplines in order to effectively engage with these specialists in multidisciplinary teams, as well as help to educate them in data analysis.

Figure 1.1 Data analysis disciplines

Data Analysis Disciplines
Change Management Project Management Business Analysis

Statistics & Machine Learning Descriptive Statistics Predictive Statistics Machine Learning	**Data Manipulation** Data Extraction DataTransformation Data Loading

One way of addressing knowledge gaps is to reach out and engage in training, communication and knowledge sharing with these communities.

ADVANCES IN COMPUTER SCIENCE

In the past few decades various areas of computer science have given us great developments in technological capabilities to store, process and analyse data. However, many of these developments demand new knowledge and skills to enable analysts to efficiently utilise them.

Emergence of Big Data

The data that is available for data analysis continues to grow rapidly and the term 'Big Data' has emerged to describe this development. The term was coined in 2001 by Doug Laney (2001), and it draws attention to three Vs that characterise the challenges that this new data poses.

- **Volume:** the amount of data collected is becoming too big for traditional storage solutions.
- **Velocity:** the speed with which data has to be processed exceeds traditional processing capabilities.
- **Variety:** the lack of an information structure required by traditional data analysis methods.

All these factors are continually challenging the traditional tools that have been used for data analysis. To meet these challenges, over recent decades there have been significant developments in new tools and techniques that can efficiently address the challenges of Big Data. However, many of these tools and techniques require new specialist knowledge by the data analysts that operate them.

The Internet of Things and digitalisation

The emergence of Big Data challenges come partly from a growing trend popularly referred to as the Internet of Things (IoT), wherein previously mechanical equipment is turned into computer-controlled internet devices, such as phones, white goods, cars, watches and so on. These devices are able to generate a large amount of data that is increasingly easy to capture and store for analysis. The data generated by these devices, together with speed and lack of traditional structure, are all contributing to the Big Data challenges faced by analysts.

Analytical technology and tools are also challenged by the growing amount of unstructured data that is available, such as natural language text.

> **WHAT IS STRUCTURED AND UNSTRUCTURED DATA?**
>
> Structured data is organised in a predetermined format. It is often stored in database tables or other systems that ensure it conforms to a specific arrangement that typically suits computer analysis.
>
> Unstructured data is not arranged so that it suits computer analysis. It can be natural language text, images or other formats that are typically aimed at humans and difficult for computers to analyse.

Natural language text information comes partly from the digitalisation of previously paper-based records and partly from collected emails, social media records, blogs and so on. The information contained in this data is very accessible to a human reader, but it's challenging to design algorithms that enable computers to access this information.

ADVANCES IN DATA STORAGE

The physical cost of data storage has dramatically decreased over the past few decades and this has enabled the storage of ever-increasing amounts of data. The use of outsourced data storage solutions, also known as cloud storage, and the use of distributed data storage solutions has been expanding to accommodate this demand.

WHAT IS DISTRIBUTED STORAGE AND CLOUD?

Distributed storage is when data is stored across several computers in a network. These systems can increase the amount of data that can be stored and the speed with which it can be accessed. A common system for distributed storage is cloud solutions, where data is accessed via the internet. This can also bring the benefit of being able to access data from any machine connected to the internet and means that the data is still available even after the failure of a local computer.

The changing nature of the data used for data analysis has both been facilitated by and required advancements in our data storage solutions. The traditional relational databases, which are characterised by the use of Structured Query Language (SQL), have been challenged by the rise of non SQL (or not only SQL; NoSQL) alternatives. These solutions are designed to be more efficient and intuitive to use on unstructured textual data. However, they often require the use of different query languages to extract and process the data. Relational databases, SQL and NoSQL alternatives are covered in more detail in Chapter 3.

FREE, PUBLIC AND OPEN DATA

As briefly mentioned earlier, there is a growing amount of free, open and public data available for data analysis from a variety of online sources. The UK government is leading this trend with its data.gov.uk website initiative where thousands of free data sets are provided about public services, demographics and democracy. This creates immense opportunities for analysts to gain deeper insights.

However, the integration of such data sets also creates a great challenge. They need to be organised so that they can be integrated into the structure of existing data and reports that the organisation has access to. This requires analysts to understand how this data has been accumulated and summarised.

ADVANCES IN DATA PROCESSING

There have also been great improvements in the ability to process the growing volumes of data and to handle the increasing complexity of this data. These improvements have come both from progress in the ability to process data in-memory, as opposed to reading and writing data to disk between processing steps, as well as the emergence of parallel processing capabilities.

Parallel hardware improvements

Using parallel processing to increase the speed with which data can be processed is nothing new, but recent years have seen the maturity and wider commercial use of a number of advanced techniques. One of these is the switch from exclusively using central processing units (CPUs) to using units designed for graphical processing (GPUs). These processing units are specifically built to perform calculations on many data points at once and, with the right techniques, can help significantly in processing Big Data volumes.

Parallel cooperating clusters

The parallel processing trend that has emerged involves the use of collections of low specification, relatively cheap, commodity computers that each process a small subset of a larger calculation. In these setups, the individual computers are referred to as nodes and a collection of them is referred to as a cluster. The most successful system for managing such clusters is the open source Apache Hadoop system and its closely related relatives. However, this system has a new programming paradigm and requires an understanding of the techniques that it employs, thus demanding more specialist knowledge from data analysts.

ADVANCES IN STATISTICAL AND MACHINE LEARNING

The past few decades have also seen rapid developments in statistical analysis techniques, which have been both enabled by computational science developments and driven the demand for more developments. Traditional statistical analysis methods have required data to be in a tabular structure where each row is an independent observation. We are now seeing new techniques to analyse data that does not adhere to this strict format.

These techniques are being expanded with machine learning algorithms that are often inspired by biological processes and apply a pragmatic approach to finding hidden information. The implementation of these algorithms poses a challenge to data analysts, who need to both understand and employ the new techniques associated with them.

Machine learning

The field of data mining has brought in new techniques that use computers to get insights from very large data sets. These are often referred to as machine learning techniques, and include both supervised and unsupervised methods.

Supervised learning methods use a data set with a number of characteristics and a target variable that the system is trained to predict. When the system is subsequently presented with the characteristics, it will make a prediction as to the expected value of the target variable. Such methods are popular when companies want to predict a future or unknown outcome, such as whether an applicant is likely to repay a loan.

> **WHAT IS A VARIABLE?**
>
> A variable is a singular value that is stored, manipulated and used in a computer program. It can contain information such as a number, a text string, a date and so on.

Unsupervised learning methods are used to find patterns in a large data set where the existence or nature of these patterns is not known. There are many areas where these techniques have been used, which range from finding out if a data set contains groups of similar records, to detection of anomalies.

Natural language processing

Within the last decade or two we have seen a rapid increase in the amount of unstructured textual data that is being captured and stored. Natural language processing has emerged as a very popular discipline for the analysis of textual data. The techniques that are being deployed for this type of analysis depend on the computational processing and storage capabilities that are available to data analysts. This is another analysis task that data analysts need to get to grips with.

Visualisation

In data analysis, the ability to display information in an easily understandable manner has always been important for efficient exploration. However, with growing volumes of data and the more complex formats that data takes, the ability to graphically explore and deliver information is business-critical. This has led to the development of a variety of data visualisation tools and techniques that are able to convey data in an intuitive and visually appealing way. These tools often require some knowledge on the part of the analyst about how best to effectively communicate complex ideas to non-technical people. Visualisation is a very useful, often a necessary, skill for data analysts to have.

The emergence of data science

The role 'data scientist' was touted as the 'sexiest' job of the 21st century in 2012 (Davenport and Patil 2012). Not surprisingly, this has led to a large growth of educational programmes that cater to data science and an even bigger increase in people having this job title or self-describing as such. However, the definition of the discipline of data science and the skills that the practitioners in this field need to have continue to be the subject of intense debate.

Opinions on what defines a data scientist range from covering only people that employ the scientific method when working with data, to everyone that works with data exploration. The attitude of applying the scientific method of making observations and testing hypotheses when working with large data sets might be an important attitude, but not one that describes the skills needed for data science.

Most business leaders consider the successful application of the data science discipline to require skills in manipulating data with programming, drawing inferences with statistics or machine learning techniques and the ability to influence decision-makers by effectively communicating the analytical results. All of these skills are needed to effectively extract, manipulate and communicate data, and experts in unstructured techniques often need to cooperate with experts in structured techniques.

There is a significant overlap between data science and data analysis, although it is more common to use the title 'data science' to describe people that apply machine learning instead of statistics, and work with unstructured rather than 'old-fashioned' data sources.

LEGAL AND ETHICAL CONSIDERATIONS FOR DATA ANALYSIS

Organisations have for a long time been aware of the value that can be gained from using the data they own. The data that these organisations own and have responsibility for will need to be managed stringently in order to comply with the growing number of laws and regulations as well as increasing public focus on how data is used. Due to privacy concerns related to mishandling or misuse of data, organisations are now facing increasingly tighter restrictions on how they can use the data they gather.

Data analysts will need to have knowledge of data management and governance so that they can comply with these requirements. This area is increasingly complex and will be discussed in much greater depth in Chapter 4. This section will merely introduce the subject in a broader context.

General Data Protection Regulation

There have been regulations in the UK to protect the use of data since the 1980s and these have grown considerably over the years. The legal and regulatory complexities come from both the breadth and depth of the laws within different countries, but also from the differences that exist between them. There have been a number of initiatives to harmonise laws and regulations between countries, with the latest being the General Data Protection Regulation (GDPR), which has been created by and applies to the European Union (EU). This lists six principles for data protection that apply to personal data attributed to a single individual:

- lawful, fair and transparent processing;
- specific, explicit and legitimate purpose;
- adequate, relevant and limited data;
- accurate data;
- kept no longer than necessary;
- processed and stored securely.

This regulation defines a separate classification for information containing sensitive personal data that can only be processed in very limited and specific circumstances.

Data privacy concerns

There is an ongoing and intense debate about who owns data, what can be done with it and how we can ensure that it is kept safe. This debate has sprung from the realisation that data presents an incredible amount of knowledge, much of it personal, and gives a great deal of influence to the people that have access to it and the ability to analyse it.

There are a growing number of organisations, both public and private, that are able to make automated personalised services, such as purchase suggestions and targeted advertising, based on algorithms that have access to detailed data about individuals. These personalised services are popular with some groups but also very unpopular with others, and it can be difficult to satisfy both sides.

There is a tension between the progress that can be made by implementing new, advanced data analysis, contrasted with the expectations of privacy that the public has. It is important that data analysts and the IT community adhere to ethical guidelines and working practices, alongside relevant laws and regulations, that will accommodate both of these attitudes.

Security

The secure storage and processing of data is a growing concern, which is in part driven by the increasing amount of data protection regulation that imposes severe penalties in cases of non-compliance, but also by the implementation of cloud solutions. Implementation of cloud solutions results in organisational data being geographically spread out across many locations, and these locations might not be controlled by the organisations themselves, which makes the protection of the data they hold more complex.

When an organisation controls the location where the data is secured, then they can focus on securing its 'border' with the outside world. With cloud solutions, this 'border' perimeter becomes much less defined, and organisations increasingly rely on internal security measures for data protection.[6]

These security measures often involve a combination of encrypting data so that it is not able to be read outside the

---

[6] For further details see Sutton 2017.

organisation and providing various forms of access control to databases and systems.

Although the design and maintenance of information security systems is normally outside the responsibilities of a data analyst, they will often be very significantly influenced by these systems. They will therefore greatly benefit from having a good understanding of both the techniques used in this field and familiarising themselves with the security policies in place in their organisation.

Decision transparency

There is a growing trend for regulators and the public to demand information about the reasons behind a decision that affects them. There is often consternation among customers when they are given, or notice, an unexplained analytical decision.

This is exemplified by a comedy sketch in the TV show *Little Britain* in which a member of the public approaches a customer service agent with a request, which is then keyed into a computer. The agent subsequently turns to the customer and, expressionless, responds 'computer says no'.

To meet these expectations, data analysts need to consider carefully how they design the models that they are using. When models are used to make a recommendation, these may need to be accompanied by the data used to make the decision and enough explanation for a customer or member of staff to interpret it.

This can pose specific problems with regard to types of models that are particularly difficult to interpret, such as some modern machine learning techniques. Data analysts will therefore need to be aware and knowledgeable about how to explain their results to non-analytical colleagues, customers and, occasionally, members of the public.

HOW THE IT INDUSTRY CAN ADDRESS THE CHALLENGES OF DATA ANALYSIS

As this chapter has explained, there are many challenges that the IT industry faces with respect to data analysis. This section will merely mention five important areas; these should by no means be taken as an exhaustive list.

Making IT (and data analysis) good for society

BCS, The Chartered Institute for IT is committed to the vision of 'Making IT good for Society', which is written into its charter.

The institute is focused on addressing four key challenges, of which data analysis has a crucial role to contribute to each.

Challenge: education
In education, it is their goal to ensure that every child has the opportunity to learn computer science. With the role of data in society becoming ever more prevalent, it is essential that children learn and understand how data is analysed. Some children will grow up to perform this analysis, but all children will be affected by data and should therefore have a fundamental understanding of its principles.

Challenge: health and social care
In health and social care, the institute wants to bring people together and create an environment that focuses on individuals. The amount of data that the health and social care industry records about people is growing very rapidly. It is easy for data analysts to become captivated by the endless possibilities to improve conditions through sophisticated analytical methods, but it is vital that we do not lose sight of the individual people behind the mountains of data that is collected.

Challenge: personal data
In personal data, the institute aims to ensure that individual data works not just for organisations, but also for people and society. The data that is collected about us and our daily lives has great value for organisations and their ability to provide us

with a personalised service. This can bring benefits to both the organisations and to the people they serve, but it is important that this data is shared legally, ethically and fairly.

Challenge: capability

In capability, the institute works to provide the skills that individuals need to enable them to do great work, in the right roles and as part of strong teams. Analysis of data requires both advanced individual technical skills and for us to work in diverse interdisciplinary teams. It is therefore equally important that, as data analysts, we both improve our technical competencies and engage and improve our relationship with other professions.

Technical challenges

There are many technical challenges faced by the IT and data analysis communities to keep up with the increasing amounts of data and changes in the way that we relate to our data. This section cannot describe them all, but will merely draw attention to one that is of specific importance to the changing skill set of data analysts.

The IT profession cannot and should not be alone in addressing all the challenges that face data analysis. Data analysis is a cross-discipline approach involving professionals in related fields such as statistics, machine learning, project management, business analysis and communication. Data analysts need to work together with these specialists to address challenges such as those mentioned above.

Traditionally, data has been stored and analysed in a tabular format, with rows representing unrelated observations. This is usually done using a relational database management system (RDBMS) which is accessed with SQL. There have been many decades of research into the efficient handling of such data and development of commercial technical solutions.

However, we are seeing a rising amount of data and specialised analytical solutions that do not fit this format, such as textual data and social media network data. This creates technical challenges for the IT profession to develop ways of storing, processing and analysing data that are as efficient and effective as the traditional methods.

This challenge is being met by development and research into alternative storage solutions, which are often known as NoSQL databases. Data analysts need to be aware of these systems as they often require different data extraction and manipulation skills from those for traditional systems. Chapter 3 provides an expanded introduction to NoSQL systems.

Ethics of data analysis

BCS, The Chartered Institute for IT sets out four ethical standards in its Code of Conduct, which describe the minimum expectations for its members. These standards have a high relevance to data analysis, whether one is a member of BCS or not, and can be used as a guideline for data analysis professionals. The descriptions below are not a comprehensive coverage of the code, but merely show that the issues it raises are highly pertinent to the activities of data analysis.[7]

Public interest
It is important that data analysts are aware of how to keep data, especially personal information about members of the public, secure from unauthorised access. They also need to know how to ensure that the results of the analysis do not negatively impact those about whom the data is collected. These are some of the important principles of the GDPR, which is described in more detail in Chapter 4.

Professional competence and integrity
The area of data analysis is broad and covers many skills and competencies. It is important that analysts keep improving their knowledge and engage in continuous professional development in order to stay relevant.

---
[7] You can see the full BCS Code of Conduct here: www.bcs.org/category/6030

Duty to relevant authority

Data analysts are often in possession of important knowledge that can be very valuable to both to the organisation in which they are employed and to people who do not have legitimate access to that data. It is important that analysts are vigilant about data protection and are aware of the obligations that organisations such as the Information Commissioner's Office in the UK put on organisations that use personal data.

Duty to the profession

It is important for data analysis as a profession, as well as for the reputation of data analysis as a discipline, for data analysts to maintain a high level of professional integrity and responsibility at all times.

Another code of conduct that is relevant to data analysts is that used by the Royal Statistical Society.[8]

Democratisation of data access

The insights that come from analysis of the data generated by public institutions has always had great importance for the democratic debate. Political interest groups that are able to demonstrate their agenda with economic or demographic data (such as unemployment, health care, the use of libraries, roadwork schedules, etc.) demand more attention in newspapers, TV broadcasts and social media than those that are not so able. It is not surprising, therefore, that the data these institutions hold is increasingly seen as an asset that belongs to the public and should therefore be freely available.

The UK government is leading the way in making large data sets available via the internet with the data.gov.uk initiative, where thousands of detailed data sets are available. These data sets cover a wide range of areas concerning local councils, national agencies and governmental departments. The data

---

[8] See www.rss.org.uk/RSS/Join_the_RSS/Code_of_conduct/RSS/Join_the_RSS/Code_of_conduct.aspx

is available to freely download to improve knowledge about how these institutions work, but also for use in commercial enterprises.

Explaining data analysis to the public

As data analysts, we have an important role to play in ensuring public and political debate stays informed and factual. The insights that come from the analysis of data can reveal complex information, but are sometimes counter-intuitive to both data analysts and other stakeholders, although they may contain very valuable information. This can be difficult enough to communicate to professional managers, but may present a real challenge when the audience is politicians or the public. Such audiences could have a significant interest in how the results can affect them, but might not have extensive, or any, experience of the topic and background of the analysis. When the results are controversial, it can present a major challenge to present them clearly, objectively and with impact in a debate, especially one dominated by social media and which demands simplicity and brevity.

To ensure that data continues to inform an objective public debate, the analytical community needs to continue to improve the ability to communicate both the results and the methods that are used in data analysis. To help us in achieving this, we need to work with journalists and technical educators as well as improve our own skills in these subjects. It is encouraging to see the rising trend of journalists that specialise in scrutinising and communicating analytical knowledge, part of a discipline known as data journalism. As data analysts, it is important that we encourage this trend and engage with this community of journalists.

SUMMARY

This chapter has provided an overview of the current state of the data analysis discipline. This is a very big discipline that requires knowledge of statistics, machine learning and data manipulation, among other areas. It is also a discipline that touches business, non-profit organisations and public services alike.

The wide-ranging skills and the complex specialities involved in data analysis are continually challenging those in this profession. It is therefore necessary that data analysts have a broad and constantly developing skill set. This skill set, and the mentality needed to keep developing it, is the subject of the next chapter.

2 THE ROLE OF DATA ANALYST

This chapter is designed to explain the profile of a data analyst, their role within a strategic organisation and the knowledge and skills needed by an analyst to contribute positively to the challenges of the analytical business environment. This chapter particularly focuses on the soft skills and competencies of an analyst's role.

WHAT IS A DATA ANALYST?

A data analyst is someone who analyses data to find patterns, trends or hidden information and translates these into insights that can be useful to business. It is a critical role in modern organisations.

Data analysts make sense of the noise that exists in data: they aggregate and translate this data into relevant business metrics and analyse it to provide meaningful insights relevant to their organisation's decision-making needs.

A successful analyst becomes integral to strategic decision-making and can grow his or her career into critical business roles within business intelligence and strategic planning. Analysts can be from a variety of educational backgrounds. While there is no mandatory qualification required to become a data analyst, a degree in computing, mathematics, statistics, economics or research is helpful. Analysts also benefit from education and experience in fields as diverse as sociology, humanities, marketing, engineering or other research degrees.

AFFILIATED ROLES AND DIFFERENCES

Data storage architecture and warehousing became popular in the 1980s. Early on, the focus was on storing data efficiently only for the purpose of producing basic management reporting. Since then, data analysis has come a long way and there are now various roles that support data-driven initiatives in an organisation. Roles have been created as the use of data has evolved and the complexity of managing and leveraging data has increased.

Nearly all data-related roles have some overlap; some of the key data roles are shown and described in Figure 2.1. Data analysts should collaborate and work with these other roles.

Figure 2.1 Key data-related roles and differences

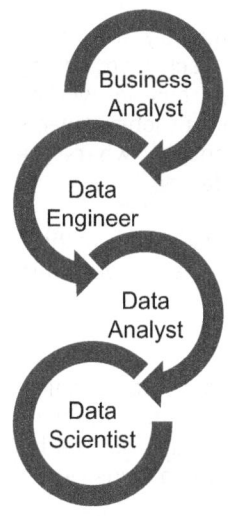

Business Analyst — Tasked with analysing business systems, identifying options for improvement and ensuring the effective implementation of information systems to help deliver organisational goals

Data Engineer — Responsible for designing, creating and maintaining databases and other large-scale data processing systems

Data Analyst — Involved in data extraction, analysis and generating insights from data to solve business problems

Data Scientist — Organises and cleans Big Data, builds models and generates insights through analysis and statistics

KEY INDUSTRIES WHERE DATA ANALYSTS WORK

The role of data analyst is not limited to any particular industry. However, some of the key industries where data analysts thrive are:

- aviation;
- banking;
- consumer goods;
- government enterprises;
- insurance;
- IT;
- manufacturing;
- market research;
- pharmaceuticals;
- social media and communications;
- telecoms;
- utilities.

Industry-specific knowledge requirements

There are not necessarily any specific industry knowledge requirements that hold a data analyst back from taking up a role in an industry where the analyst has not worked previously. It may be beneficial for the analyst's job prospects to have experience of working in the industry where the vacancy exists, but this is not always mandatory.

To be successful in the job, a data analyst needs a mix of three main types of skills: functional, technical and soft (see Figure 2.2). These are explained in detail later in this chapter, with a particular focus on the role of soft skills.

If an analyst is able to migrate functional and technical skills across different industries, and invest in continually developing these along with targeted soft skills needed for that organisation, they can easily move between industries.

As an example, an analyst working in insurance with advanced mathematical knowledge can target the IT industry based on existing functional and technical skills, but will need to become familiar with the business challenges particular to IT setups.

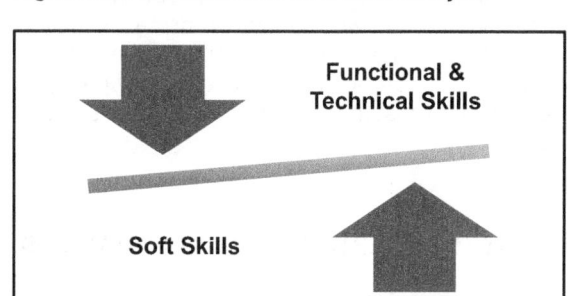

Figure 2.2 Skills needed as a data analyst

> A Data Analyst with an understanding of business is the perfect catalyst for developing true knowledge on which to reliably base commercial success.
> (Michael Collins, Managing Consultant, Database Marketing Counsel)

Certain industries, and specific roles within them, might require certain knowledge or aptitude. A credit risk data analyst, for instance, might be well versed with the regulations relating to Basel norms,[1] but might not have the necessary skills to work with documenting the results of a clinical trial in the pharmaceutical industry. While it is impossible for a candidate to know all the nuances of each industry, a general understanding of how an industry operates is often critical to be able to transition across roles in various industries with ease.

---

[1] The Basel committee was established by 10 leading countries in 1974 to deal with problems in the financial world. It publishes norms that most central banks follow to manage their credit policy.

> For a generic guide on skills and their application in the industry, the Skills Framework for the Information Age (SFIA)[2] is a helpful guide. Among its multiple benefits, the SFIA can help a data analyst in resource planning, deployment and assessment of team members for various roles.

NATURE OF TASKS UNDERTAKEN BY DATA ANALYSTS

A data analyst is usually involved in solving business problems specific to the challenges faced by the industry they are in, or problems emanating from the life cycle that a particular organisation works with. For example:

- At the start of the 21st century, most data analysts working within the IT sector or the IT arm of any organisation were heavily involved with data interpretation related to the Y2K[3] issue that threatened to stop all computers from functioning.
- Data analysts working in the banking industry may be engaged in assessing customer brand satisfaction by analysing feedback, queries, complaints and other comments and activities done by customers.
- Data analysts in the automotive sector are often engaged in collecting and analysing data to bring in innovations such as cleaner, smarter and self-driven vehicles.

These are examples of industry level problems that analysts can be engaged in. They may vary widely between organisations within the same industry, depending on the life cycle within that industry.

---

[2] More information can be found at www.sfia-online.org/en

[3] The term for a class of computer bugs, relating to the storage of calendar dates for the dates beginning in the year 2000, that threatened to stop computers functioning normally.

Let's explore the various stages of a product's life cycle within an organisation (see Figure 2.3) and the typical tasks that a data analyst might be undertaking within these life cycle stages.

Figure 2.3 Typical product life cycle

Ideation ❯ Growth stage ❯ Maturity ❯ Challenges ❯ Relaunch or Phase out

- **Ideation:** insight generation and data mining to support project scope; write up of the target product profile; analysis of inputs from various customers; and preparing the commercial business case for the new idea/product.

- **Growth stage:** supporting product growth strategies; driving better connection with customers; mining data insights to support issue redressal regarding product design, support offered and so on; and implementing strategies to ensure sustained growth of the product.

- **Maturity:** supporting internal and external strategy development to maximise return on investment, while experiencing sustained market share but slower growth.

- **Challenges:** using market feedback data to evaluate the next available options for a product in the face of growing competition, lack of user interest, pricing challenges, product/service becoming obsolete, or slower growth.

- **Relaunch/Phase-out:** implementing the decisions that have been taken as a result of data analysis; analysing product performance versus original business case and in-market metrics; and working with business intelligence and finance teams to deliver the analysis to relevant decision-makers.

Availability of data and its impact on an analyst's scope of work

The amount of data available can influence the way data analysts approach problems. Take the examples below, for instance.

Let's say an organisation currently in the growth stage of a product is trying to deal with the poor app performance that its users are facing. In such a scenario it is likely that there is abundant data available on the usage of the app and the specifics of when the users experience issues. The analyst, in this case, has data to analyse and can help to identify the reason for the problems.

In another scenario, let's assume the same product is dealing with low usage issues. How can the analyst try and understand the reasons for low usage? If there were multiple segments of users of the app, with some heavy and some light users, the analyst could try to profile both segments to gain insights. In such an instance, the analyst will have to collaborate extensively with the business teams involved and try to check various hypotheses on why the usage is lower than expected. The analyst will also have to check if any of the team members have been receiving qualitative feedback, and could suggest that the business conduct a primary research survey and seek feedback on user experiences if necessary.

Even in a scenario with abundant data, the data analyst may try and incorporate additional sources of information to analyse. If the analyst is analysing sales growth in the past year and trying to make sense of the forecasts generated for the next few quarters, they may try and include data about the macroeconomic parameters published by the central bank.

While designing a new process to screen the eligibility of applicants, a data analyst may suggest that it could be useful to approach one of the leading credit bureaus to seek further information about the applicant and use it to augment the data already held by the company.

DATA ANALYST KEY RESPONSIBILITIES

The responsibilities of a data analyst depend on the industry and organisation they are working within, and are also influenced by the level of investment in data their organisation makes. Broadly, these are the key responsibilities of a data analyst:

- Extracting data using relevant software and code.
- Analysing data to generate insights.
- Transforming these insights into simple, easy to understand information for stakeholders, with the help of data visualisation tools.

Extraction

This usually entails extracting data for reports and projects that the data analyst is tasked with producing. Certain business events may also trigger a request for customised data extraction.

Analysis

The data analyst would then generate insights based on the data and the business understanding. Inputs from subject matter experts (SMEs) may be required at this stage. Some insights from the data may be counter-intuitive to expectations and this could be a result of data quality issues or a gap in business understanding of the problem. SME involvement would help to corroborate the insights generated.

Transformation

The data analyst can then share the insights with stakeholders using a data visualisation tool. Data visualisation entails using tables, graphs or other measures to present the data insights in a clear, visual manner. Seldom would the analyst present insights without some form of data visualisation.

> Successful data analysis depends on the data analyst's understanding of the organisation and processes that have generated the data. This understanding is needed so they can choose what types of analytical techniques are most appropriate for the tasks at hand and to help them explain the analytical results to the interested parties. This understanding is generated by efficient business analysis, which in larger projects can be undertaken by trained specialists but often must be done by the data analysts themselves. It is therefore important that data analysts understand business analysis and are able to systematically understand complex organisations. In larger projects with professional business analysts, it is also important that they are able to interpret the documentation, models and technology used by business analysts to collaborate efficiently.

> Data Analyst as a key role is about getting the real business value from blind data for the right audience. To put the key data pieces into the right context and structure.
> (Martin Florian, Head of Capco Advisory, The Capital Markets Company)

DATA ANALYST KEY SKILLS

As mentioned earlier in this chapter, an analyst needs a blend of three types of skills to be successful: functional, technical and soft skills.

- **Functional skills** can be defined as those learned at school, such as reading, writing, language, mathematics and computer usage abilities. Advanced level functional skills can be acquired through university education or specialist institutional degrees.

- **Technical skills** are specialist skills relating to technology. For an analyst, these are a mix of proficiency with data centric software (SAS, SQL, etc.), extraction, transformation and loading (ETL) skills and analytics skills.

- **Soft skills**, covered in detail later, are more intangible skills that relate to personal attributes. For a data analyst, they mainly revolve around understanding of the industry and organisational business challenges.

This chapter focuses on soft skills to highlight the importance of these skills in the role of data analyst. When dealing with experts with similar technical skills, the only distinguishing factor among these experts could be their soft skills.

Key functional skills

- At least GCSE Maths and English knowledge: basic knowledge of these subjects is assumed for data analysts.
- An appreciation of statistic, business and finance knowledge, and an understanding of IT and data: this understanding can be acquired through higher education, training workshops and on-the-job learning opportunities.

Key technical skills

- **Ability to create and understand complex data structures:** a typical database consists of hundreds of tables with various data dimensions. Date and product are just two examples of the tens of dimensions of data into which tables could be organised. Some tables may be linked with customer or various other identifiers. The data analyst needs to understand such complex data structures to be able to successfully query and retrieve the required information. Furthermore, the data analyst could be required to create localised versions of these data structures to enable additional analysis without the need to repeatedly query the main database.

- **Programming language skills to enable the extraction of data from the data warehouse and other sources** (for example, VBA, SQL, Hive, Hadoop, Impala, etc.): these skills are a prerequisite to extract data; the data analyst might be required to write their own code, or rerun existing code after acquiring at least a basic understanding of the code structure and steps to resolve common issues faced in running an existing piece of code.

- **Ability to handle a large volume of data:** the data analyst should be able to identify the data subset relevant to the business problem. This might entail joining multiple tables, aggregating data and deploying the right exclusion criteria. These actions need to be performed by leveraging procedures that enable faster processing. Each task rerun on a large volume of data would substantially increase the overall timelines for task delivery.

- **Experience of working with statistical software to analyse data** (for example, MATLAB, R, SAS): statistical software has inbuilt procedures and/or provides the capability to write queries that help to assess data quality. The data analyst should use this capability to analyse data and also to help rectify issues with the data. Prior to handing over the data insights to stakeholders, it is always best practice to run some data quality checks to ensure that reliable data insights are handed over.

- **Advanced Microsoft Excel skills:** data might be presented to data analysts in an Excel spreadsheet. VBA coding may be required to access data or pivot tables may be needed to visualise data analysis results.

Key soft skills

Data analysts need a variety of soft skills in line with the tasks they perform on a daily basis. These include the ability to deal with challenges, stakeholder management, maintaining multiple communication channels and presenting results. Figure 2.4 lists some data analyst key tasks and associated soft skills.

Figure 2.4 Key tasks and soft skills required

Dealing with challenges
- adaptability
- adjusting to a learning curve
- ethics

Communication
- establishing communication channels
- keeping the audience engaged
- feedback

Stakeholder management
- listening
- analytical thinking
- negotiation skills
- conflict resolution
- problem-solving

Presentation
- understand the audience
- articulation
- raising the team profile

Task management
- time management
- priortisation
- decision-making

Let's look at these skills in more detail.

Dealing with challenges

Some of the challenges that a data analyst faces emanate from data issues, processes, stakeholders and systems. The analyst can deal with challenges by working on the following soft skills.

Adaptability   As the Greek philosopher Heraclitus is reputed to have said: change is the only constant. A data analyst needs to be prepared for change. Whether finding solutions to business problems, or business process engineering to create a new or improved process, a data analyst is constantly involved in change.

A data analyst seldom deals with the same problem over a long period of time. Even if the problem remains the same for some time, the data and its inherent message keep constantly evolving.

As an example, data analysts working for telecom companies over the last couple of decades would have noticed changes in the business environment. From being an item of luxury or convenience, the mobile phone has now become a necessity. Voice calls are not the primary purpose of these devices any more: messaging and internet usage are the predominantly used functions. Data captured in this instance would highlight the change in customer behaviour. Mobile operators have had to adapt by changing the tariffs offered as a result of data analysis of customer behaviour.

Not all change is the outcome of industry changes or customer behaviour. Some change may be forced by regulators. Either way, a data analyst has to be prepared for continual change.

Adjusting to learning curves For a data analyst, the learning never stops.

Data at one point, in the infancy stage of computing and digital storage, was stored on floppy disks and exchanged among various teams and businesses. Not all aspects of a customer's banking transactions were digitally recorded prior to the advent of core banking systems. These days, every aspect of a customer's interaction with an organisation is recorded and can be analysed. It is quite normal to hear the voice on a bank's phone menu say that all calls may be recorded for monitoring or training purposes. Every click on a grocery retailer's website is recorded to help analyse customer behaviour.

A data analyst needs to constantly learn new skills and adjust to a steep learning curve in the shortest time possible to deal with various changes in the industry. The process of retrieving data, assimilating it, making inferences and sharing the results has undergone a lot of automation in recent years and has also been the subject of much analytical research.

THE ROLE OF DATA ANALYST

A data analyst needs to be aware of the technologies intended to augment the daily job. While it is impossible to keep pace with all advances in the industry simultaneously, having the ability to adjust quickly to steep learning curves does no harm in maintaining standards in the workplace.

Ethics   While being ethical is in itself not a soft skill, there are various aspects of ethical behaviour at the workplace that can be developed to ensure that high standards are maintained at all times.

Ethical standards are an underlying requirement for almost everything we do in life but in the case of data analysis, these standards come to the forefront. This is because of the sensitivity of data that an analyst has access to. Prior to appointment, every data analyst would have been subjected to some level of reference checks to ensure that they can be trusted with data.

A data analyst needs to be self-aware and have the best interest of stakeholders at heart. Analysts need to understand the risks that their business processes face. They need to have the courage to escalate any issues through the right medium – be it a manager, whistleblowing helpline, law enforcement officer or whatever. Data analysts are also responsible for ensuring data integrity.

A data analyst should not be mistaken for a cybersecurity expert; however, they can still contribute to ensuring that best practices are adhered to and highlight any potential security lapses relating to data storage and access.

Data analysts can make significant contributions in the workplace by bringing a positive work ethic and dealing effectively and efficiently with any mistakes. Some mistakes made by data analysts could have far-reaching consequences. A mistake itself might be a basic error. For example, a data analyst may have utilised the wrong monthly data file to deduce insights about the passenger load in an airline. The management committee's action based on such a report may lead to significant problems. What if the data analyst realised the mistake after the insights had already been presented? Should they highlight the error? Not only does the analyst need to highlight the error, in many circumstances it is the analyst and the related team that need to produce a new set of figures and related inferences, and quickly. The error might have been caused by some inconsistent messaging from the management team itself; however, even if this is the case, the data analyst needs to raise a hand and highlight the error and then try and help to fix the fallout from the situation.

Stakeholder management
Managing stakeholders can be a difficult task. For example, consider the importance of communication with stakeholders in the production of a brief for a new data analysis project.

Prior to investing any meaningful time to solve a business problem, data analysts need to understand the brief. A well-structured brief contains background, describes the business problem and often mentions an expectation of how the output should look. If stakeholders have not shared a brief, then the data analyst can always put one together and share it with the stakeholders, getting their feedback to ensure that the problem is understood correctly.

A lot of projects fail to deliver when the brief is not shared, is ambiguous in defining the problem and/or the expected solution is not well understood by the data analyst. In certain business situations, the brief might be ambiguous initially, but after some analysis and preliminary insights, the data analyst can work with stakeholders to rewrite it.

This section will cover the key soft skills that data analysts need in order to deal effectively with stakeholders.

Listening This is not the same as hearing, which is a physical attribute. If a data analyst is a good listener, the analyst would accurately understand what is being said and interpret the message correctly.

Listening includes both verbal and non-verbal messaging. At times, the body language of stakeholders is important when the business problem is being described. For example, leaning in can indicate that they are interested and actively listening. Slouching in a chair in a meeting, however, may indicate that they are in passive mode or, worse, uninterested.

Some people are keen to reply rather than listen. By listening, a data analyst is trying to process as much information as possible. In certain business scenarios, the business problem might have already been partially worked on by another set of analysts. In this case, the data analyst needs to understand the progress made by other individuals in attempting to solve the problem.

Listening is also important for an analyst to perform a role within a team. Whether a team leader or team member, a data analyst has to actively listen and take on board multiple views, for instance while conducting focus group discussions to understand customer preferences. A lot of business metrics have also evolved around listening. Net promoter score (NPS)[4] and voice of customer (VOC)[5] are examples of such metrics.

Analytical thinking Data analysts must apply analytical thinking and conduct critical reviews. Going back to the example of the project brief mentioned in the introduction to this section, analytical thinking is necessary to understand it fully and refine it if appropriate. Often, stakeholders are unable to give structured requirements or understand if the solution being proposed is achievable. If this is the case, data analysts should come up with a project brief themselves prior to analysis, and be clear with stakeholders what the expected results will be.

Data analysts also need to have a critical mindset when being asked to conduct analysis; they should only be investing time

---

[4] This segregates customers into promoters, passive supporters and detractors, based on customer experience, and helps to predict business growth.

[5] This is a term used by a section of industry for a process that captures customers' expectations and preferences.

in the analysis that makes sense from a logical point of view. At times, a data analyst is the only expert on the subject being discussed and it becomes imperative that the data analyst guides the stakeholders wisely and works with them to refine the project brief. An effective data analyst also has to learn to say 'no' to pieces of work that are impractical for various reasons.

Negotiation skills These come into play as soon as a data analyst is approached with a project brief. The business may want to do a very large piece of work in the shortest time possible. The data analyst has to try to accurately estimate the time it will take to deliver the task and negotiate with the stakeholders agreed start and end dates for the analysis. At times, the negotiation may entail convincing the business to reduce the scope of the work or even sponsor resources for larger pieces of work.

Data analysts might be dependent on various other teams within an organisation to deliver a piece of work. They may have to implement service level agreements (SLAs) with various teams to ensure that there is an understanding of the lag between raising a request and receiving the required information to analyse the business problem.

> SLAs within teams exist in larger organisations and help to lay out the process by which teams make internal business as usual (BAU) requests and the escalation mechanisms to deal with urgent requests. Getting an SLA in place and agreeing to mutually favourable terms requires good negotiation skills.

Conflict resolution Data analysts have to keep working towards solving the business problems at hand while simultaneously dealing with any interpersonal or inter-departmental issues that may arise.

At times, when various departments have differing approaches to solving a problem, or conflicting priorities in the short run, disputes may arise that could affect business deliverables. Not all such conflicts can be done away with completely. Data analysts must work to minimise such conflicts and use team members within the organisation as mediators if necessary. However, the first step to resolve most conflicts should ideally be a face-to-face discussion, which is held after thinking through the issue.

Problem-solving Stakeholders look to data analysts to solve problems. This may mean that the data analyst has to deal with a whole bunch of other problems to try and solve the particular problem troubling the stakeholders.

For example, a stakeholder might require an important extract of data very quickly. A new data analyst within the team, tasked with solving the stakeholder's problem, may face issues such as getting access to the right data systems, understanding the data structure and making sense of the business processes in the new environment. Given such constraints, the data analyst is still expected to deliver results. In such circumstances, what matters is the problem-solving attitude of the data analyst. Rather than being overwhelmed with issues, the data analyst needs to try and work through each problem systematically.

The importance of saying 'no' to a brief when necessary was mentioned earlier. Having said that, however, data analysts should refrain from refusing to undertake a brief just because the problem is complex. At times, the solution may not lie with the data analyst. In such circumstances, the role of SMEs becomes important. Analysts can turn to them for advice and help in solving the problem at hand.

> A data analyst is, quite simply, someone who can solve a problem. Problems always look intractable until you quantify and break them down, and then they often look obvious. The only way you do that is through data analysis. Good data analysts do this instinctively and systematically, and as data becomes exponentially bigger and more ubiquitous, they increasingly make the world go round.
> (Peter Kennedy, MD, Accenture)

Task management

Seldom would a data analyst work on a single task at any given time. If it is a long, drawn-out project with a single business objective, the project may need various small streams of work in order to deliver the objective; hence, the ability to manage various tasks at once becomes important. In task management, time management and prioritisation skills overlap, because both of these aspects are needed to effectively deliver tasks on time. The data analyst has to determine their investment in a task based on the time available and its priority.

Ideally, tasks should be managed using some form of documentation. For instance, a Gantt chart may be used to display the project schedule and track the progress made; and a Fishbone (also known as cause and effect or Ishikawa) diagram can be used to identify the causes of a problem.

Different data analyst tasks can be viewed collectively as part of a project. When data analysts work as part of a small team, they will need to be able to manage their own projects within the requirements specified; and when they work as part of a larger project, they will need to liaise with professional project managers.

In this section we'll explore the different skills related to task management.

Time management   Data analysts need to estimate the time required for completing each task, both on a project basis and on a daily basis. At times it is not easy to come up with an estimate. In such instances, data analysts can benefit from breaking down the tasks into subtasks. Assigning a time component against each subtask can help to estimate the overall time required. Often, in the middle of a task, a data analyst might realise that the time needed to complete it is longer than the estimation. In this case, it is important to inform the stakeholders concerned, and discuss with them whether to postpone the due date accordingly or provide a simpler version of the analysis. In this case, the analyst would still need to deliver results with a sufficient degree of accuracy and quality insights.

To manage time effectively, data analysts also have to look inwards and ensure that they have a fair degree of understanding about:

- their own competency, and its effect on the time it takes to complete a task;
- their own level of motivation to overcome hurdles that might be faced;
- their own ability, and opportunities to delegate some tasks to others;
- their own capability to perform in stressful situations.

Prioritisation Data analysts may have to deal with multiple unexpected and critical requests, so effective prioritisation of tasks is necessary. The prioritisation process should be managed with stakeholders and/or the project manager. An efficient way to prioritise is to be transparent with the stakeholders. Having a published list of tasks helps stakeholders to understand the current status of tasks and any reasons why their particular tasks have not been prioritised or are taking longer than planned. This could save a lot of time and minimise potential conflicts. It is not uncommon for data analysts to host periodic meetings between various stakeholders and seek their help in prioritising tasks. At times, given the urgency of some tasks, certain stakeholders may be willing to de-prioritise their own requirements to help their peers in other teams.

Decision-making Data analysts may be presented with a problem or situation where a decision must be made regarding a process, data or some other work-related aspect. In an ideal situation, the data analyst would seek a consensus among all stakeholders prior to deciding; however, such a luxury might not be feasible, and the analyst might have to make decisions quickly.

At times, data analysts might not have detailed information, but may need to make a decision or put forth a proposal to the stakeholders based on limited information. Any significant independent decision that an analyst makes must be communicated with the stakeholders. The analyst should try and elicit a response from stakeholders for any outstanding issues at the earliest opportunity where the analyst is unable to make an independent decision.

Some of questions to consider before making any decisions are:

- What are the risks associated with each option available?
- Has a similar decision been made in the past, and what was the knowledge gained from it?
- Will it complicate the process if consensus with stakeholders is attempted rather than making a quick decision?
- Can the rationale for the decision be supported by data and any other documentation?
- Will the decision be made with absolute confidence or a lower degree of confidence?
- Is there any bias involved in the decision process?
- Can an impact assessment of the alternate courses of action be done?
- Does making a particular decision rule out the opportunity to conduct a certain type of analysis, or rule out the possibility of validating some hypotheses?

Some of the common decisions that data analysts may have to make relate to:

- the data period that should be selected for analysis;
- the cut-off dates that should be used for data processing (for instance, should previous month-end data be extracted on the first working day of the month, or should there be some lag allowed to ensure that all data is up to date?);
- data quality issues that may affect certain elements of the data;

- the benefits of using one analysis methodology over another;
- the minimum number of observations required to conduct analysis;
- the use of all of the data available, or use of just sample data for analysis;
- the nature of sampling that needs to be done;
- whether any exclusions should be applied to the data.

Communication

The complexity of the techniques used for data analysis often creates an atmosphere of mystery around the discipline, and this can create mistrust of the resulting outcomes and recommendations. Many colleagues that data analysts have to collaborate with do not have specific knowledge of the computational and statistical methods used, and data analysts are often required to explain complex ideas to non-specialists.

It can often be a temptation for analytical specialists to use technical jargon and to overemphasise the advanced techniques that they have used. This might create a sense of wonderment and admiration for the analysts among non-technical colleagues, but could also result in a reduction of the critical debate of the consequences of the analytical results.

To meet this challenge, the analytical community must improve their ability to tell the story of their results without resorting to technical jargon. The technical details of the analysis must be reserved for internal debate about the merits of specific methods within the data analysis community.

It is also important to engage with other professionals on their terms, instead of insisting that they engage on ours, to explain what implications the analytical process will have on their working practices.

In this section we will look at communication skills in further detail.

Establishing communication channels Data analysts need to decide which stakeholders need to be involved with the various sets of communications being shared about a data analysis project. Often, multiple communications about the same task may be sent out, although these may differ in granularity and frequency. It is also necessary to establish the best medium of interaction. In an environment where teams are globally spread out and may be multilingual, deciding on the channels and frequency of communication is important. Not all recipients will respond to your communications; most stakeholders are ambushed with a host of communication, and at times it might be difficult for a data analyst to ensure that their messages get through.

Some stakeholders may prefer to take a backseat and be isolated from the process of problem-solving. Other stakeholders may wish to be actively involved for the full duration of analysis to ensure that they have visibility of the process and can contribute when necessary.

Keeping the audience engaged One of the ways to keep the audience engaged on a project is to share its milestones and goals. These must be established, to keep track of achievements, and can help to maintain focus on the overall deliverables of the analysis.

Milestones and goals help to check that the project is on track to deliver as expected. Communication about them assures the stakeholders that key tasks are being completed and serves as an opportunity for everyone to feed back on the process. We mentioned earlier that at times it becomes difficult for data analysts to estimate the overall time required for analysis. By breaking the time into subtasks, or milestones and goals, analysts might be able to estimate the time required for such activities more easily and thereby calculate more accurately the overall time required for analysis. Once the milestones and goals are achieved, they can be communicated to a wider audience.

THE ROLE OF DATA ANALYST

In some projects that fail to deliver the expected results, there is a lack of appreciation of the effort invested by data analysts in pursuing those results. It is in the interests of data analysts that a hypothesis-driven approach is adopted for analysis. A hypothesis can be defined as a set of beliefs or preconceived notions about the nature of or solution to the problem that a stakeholder has. It is rare to find a business manager who does not have certain beliefs regarding why a business metric performed in a certain way or what typical customer behaviour is. As part of the analysis, data analysts can occasionally put these hypotheses to the test and also put forward their own list of hypotheses that they aim to prove or disprove. By following this approach, even if the end objective of the analysis is not met, data analysts can show the results of hypothesis testing and thereby showcase the effort involved. Stakeholders can also gain some benefit from the exercise after looking at the results of such testing.

Feedback Earlier we mentioned the need for a project brief that describes a task for the analyst and the outcome that is expected. Data analysts should use this document to assess whether all the information, data and tools needed to undertake the task are available to them. This scrutiny will enable the data analyst to provide feedback to the stakeholders, which is important in managing expectations. To be able to provide feedback effectively, data analysts should:

- consider the level of detail to be provided in the feedback;
- understand the timing and medium of sharing the feedback;
- choose the right stakeholders to share the feedback with;
- provide the right level of detail in feedback;
- decide if the feedback process needs to be formalised, with periodic exchanges of feedback and follow-up actions.

Presentation

While it might have taken days, weeks or months to complete a piece of analysis, data analysts will usually only get a small proportion of that time to present the results. Results may be presented in the form of a Microsoft PowerPoint presentation, a written document or even a set of metrics in a spreadsheet. Presentations could be given mid-project when they relate to milestones achieved, or are otherwise given at the end of a project.

During some presentations, the objective could also be to elicit feedback to incorporate in the remaining phases of analysis. Either way, what is required is the complete attention of the stakeholders. To achieve this, the presenter must understand the audience, articulate their thoughts effectively and aim to raise the team profile.

Understand the audience Data analysts should be aware of the differences in presentation style and content to a technical versus a non-technical audience. For instance, a technical audience consisting of senior management from the insight team may be interested in knowing details about data sources and issues about data quality, whereas executive management would probably be more interested in knowing about the insights from the data and the business impact of this information.

Other instances of differences in presentation style and content include presenting to specific teams such as sales, marketing, IT or HR. At times, analysts might get a mixed audience in a room. Various audience members may be interested in specific aspects of the presentation: a statistical modelling manager, for example, may be interested in the data cleansing and transformation done by the data analyst; whereas a model implementation manager may be keen to understand if the data used is going to be consistently available in the organisation so that the solutions implemented can be run seamlessly; and a stakeholder involved in governance might be looking for assurances about the process followed in maintaining the standards of the analysis.

> Any analysis presentation should start with an executive summary that highlights the key outcomes of the analysis and relates them to the analysis objective. Use of graphs and figures will be helpful, but they should only be used to add context to the presentation rather than act as mere data points. The appendix section is the place to provide detailed information so that the stakeholders interested in delving deeper into the solution can do so at their own leisure.

Some aspects that data analysts should keep in mind about their audience are:

- the educational background or technical expertise of the attendees;
- their role(s) in the organisation;
- the stake various individuals have in the analysis being presented;
- the level of detail that is expected to be shared;
- the role that attendees may have played in conducting the analysis.

Articulation Articulation relates to the ability to present complex solutions in a simple and concise manner. A well-articulated presentation showcases the clarity of thought and level of expertise that the data analyst possesses.

Data analysts often make assumptions about data and the business scenario. These assumptions need to be articulated and documented prior to sharing the final analysis outcome. The insights should be supported by data and appropriate statistical test results. The use of jargon should be avoided, unless of course the audience is well versed in the acronyms and terminology used – sometimes not using the industry terminology could be misunderstood as a lack of familiarity with key metrics and standards used within an industry.

After sharing results with stakeholders, data analysts need to:

- be open and available for any follow-up questions that might arise over the following days;
- be clear about the best medium of communication for those questions;
- ensure that the insights are interpreted properly so that their use in any strategic business decisions does not lead to unintended consequences.

Raising the team profile Data analysts should view a presentation as an opportunity to raise the profile of their team and not just a particular piece of work. Even if the stakeholders are internal, they are in effect the customers of the team and they are consuming the service that the data analysts provide. A satisfied customer will lead to a sustained level of high-quality work requests. The stakeholders should be able to view the data analysis team as SMEs.

All teams within an organisation vie for budget and quality work. Creating the right impression helps to build trust with the senior stakeholders that, with the right amount of investment in the team, the business can meet its goals effectively.

Data analysts should share technical knowledge with stakeholders when requested. This may enable stakeholders to perform some tasks by themselves, create an appreciation among them of the work involved to complete tasks and raise the profile of the team. This all is possible by:

- establishing weekly or monthly 'Q&A' sessions when stakeholders can put questions to the data analysts;
- providing workshops or courses to interested stakeholders on specific topics (for example, basic SQL, Excel, basic statistics, etc.);
- creating a central repository of code, insights and appropriate, shareable data that stakeholders can use themselves;

- volunteering to help colleagues solve complex business problems;
- participating in learning opportunities; this helps data analysts to learn new things and also provides a chance for them to participate in discussions with a wider audience.

SUMMARY

In this chapter, we reviewed the key industries where data analysts work, the affiliated roles and the differences between the data analyst role and other roles. We also looked at where the data analyst could add value during a typical product life cycle and the nature of solving business problems. Data is a key influencer in the data analyst role, and we explored the effect of varying degrees of data availability on analysis deliverables. We also discussed the three types of skills required – functional, technical and soft – and looked at soft skills in particular.

In the next chapter, we will discuss the tools, methods and techniques that data analysts need to use.

3 TOOLS, METHODS AND TECHNIQUES

Data analysts need to use a variety of tools, methods and techniques from the computing, statistics, machine learning, project management and change management disciplines to do their jobs. This chapter provides an introduction and overview of them.

> A good data analyst is a lot of small things done right – robust programming, analysis and presentation skills; error free and dependable work quality; critical reasoning skills; informed and well-read on their area or industry; flexible in their use of technology and methodology, and a good communicator. A lot of these coming together in a balanced way – and you go: Whoa! that's a great analyst I'd love to hire over and over again.
>
> (Amit Das, Founder, Think Analytics)

TOOLS

The data analysis area is crowded with tools, and there is constant innovation in existing tools as well as new tools appearing every year. In this section, tools have been grouped into three main categories, databases, programming tools and visualisation packages, but some tools have functionality in more than one category. Although there are some named examples of popular types of tools in this section, there are many more available.

Databases

Databases are systems that store collections of data, which can then be accessed and manipulated as required. The most common type has, for many decades, been RDBMSs, which store information efficiently and are structured according to the relational model.

Although many alternative types of systems have been developed to deal with data that cannot easily fit into this structure, such as those described in the section in this chapter on NoSQL databases, the relational database remains the most popular type.

Relational databases

Relational databases are built on the principles of the relational model which organises data according to the entities that the data belongs to; each entry is typically represented by a separate table.

> **WHAT IS AN ENTITY?**
>
> An entity is something that exists as itself. It can be a physical object (such as a car or a person), but it can also be abstract, such as an organisation, an account or an event. It is what we collect and store our data about.

To organise business data into entities, the properties and relationships of each entity are recorded. This is called data modelling and will be covered in more detail later in this chapter. More information on data modelling can also be found in the books listed for this chapter in the references at the end of this book.

In a relational system, data about employees, for example, would be stored in an Employee table, where each row represents a separate employee and the columns would represent all the attributes of each employee. The entities will be linked together so that it is possible to connect entities, such as connecting an employee with the department that they are allocated to. This would be done by using a common column in both the Employee and Department tables, such as the employee having the department code as one of its values.

There are numerous large, small, proprietary and free/open-source relational database systems available. Popular examples of relational database systems include IBM Db2, Oracle RDBMS, Microsoft Access, Microsoft SQL Server and MySQL.

NoSQL databases

The previous section described relational database systems that are designed to store structured data and be manipulated with SQL. However, these systems do not deal very well with data that cannot easily be structured according to the relational model. This includes data that is structured according to the object-oriented model: transactional data, social media data and textual data such as books, articles, blogs and social media posts. The last few decades have seen a rise in these types of data, and alternative database systems that are designed to deal with these types of data have been gaining popularity. Collectively they have been referred to as NoSQL.

Graph databases One of the alternatives to relational databases is a graph database where individual data elements are connected together to form a mathematical graph – see Figure 3.1. This type of database is designed with a focus on the connection between the individual elements that are stored. It is very suitable for analysis that deals with social interaction between individuals. It is extensively used in analysis of social media where the primary focus is the connections between people, but it can be used in any area where the relationships between elements are the primary focus.

There is extensive mathematical theory about such graphs, but statistical analysis of them and computational processing are not as well established as they are for relational databases. There is not a widely adopted language for querying and

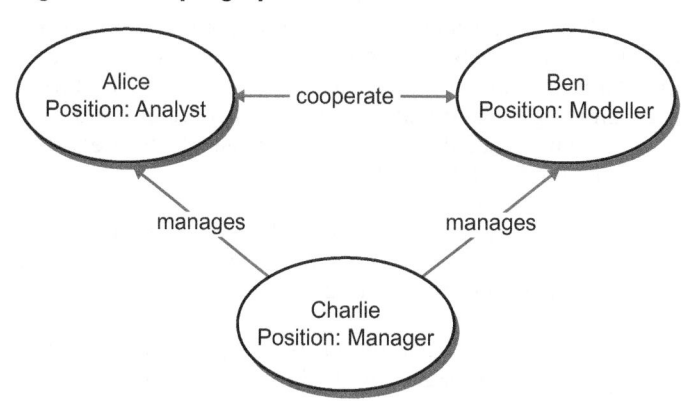

Figure 3.1 Simple graph data model

manipulating graphs either and each system therefore uses its own proprietary languages.

Popular examples of graph database systems include GraphDB and Neo4j.

Object-oriented databases In the object-oriented model, each entity is organised according to its attributes, relationships with other entities and the actions that it can undertake. Object-oriented databases are designed to directly support this data model. Although they have been in use for many decades, they are not yet as effective or as popular as relational database systems. However, they do enable more intuitive storage and retrieval of data that is organised in this way.

These databases might not support SQL, and typically use object-oriented programming languages such as Java, C# and Python to retrieve and manipulate the data that they hold.

Examples of object-oriented databases are ObjectDatabase++, Perst, ObjectDB and db4o.

Programming tools

Although code can be written using only a text editor, such as Microsoft's Notepad, most programmers will use a programming tool that provides many helpful features. Programming tools are also known as software development environments (SDEs) and usually consist of an integrated development environment (IDE).

This environment typically provides the programmer with a number of features such as a software code editor, debugging functionality, a code interpreter and a compiler.

Examples of popular programming languages for data analysis are Java, Python, R, SPSS, SAS and Matlab. The tools used for SPSS, SAS and Matlab are proprietary, specific to the languages and are usually referred to by the same names.

The Java language is popular for use with Hadoop, which combines advanced data storage and data manipulation and is used to process Big Data. The Hadoop development tools are built specifically for this purpose and normally the IDE of choice.

The Python language is a very popular choice for data analysis and there is a vast number of IDEs that can be used to write code. The Spyder IDE is part of the Anaconda distribution and is developed to work well with a number of packages specifically designed for data analysis. Other IDEs include PyCharm, which also includes features for web development, and Jupyter Notebook, which is designed for cloud computing.

R is also a popular language, particularly when dealing with sophisticated or advanced statistical data analysis. It is supported by the Anaconda distribution mentioned above, but can also be used with the R Studio and a number of other IDEs.

There is more information about the programming languages and methods used for data analysis in the following sections.

Software code editor
This SDE feature helps the programmer to write correct code. It is common for it to contain an autocorrect functionality that will guess the words as the analyst types them, similar to what is done in smartphones and tables for dictionary words. It often also lists the different arguments that the function takes so it can be assured that they are all provided. If there are any potential errors in the code, the editor might highlight or mark the relevant code, similar to spell checkers in text documents.

Debugging functionality
This feature can assist the analyst in finding errors in the code. It will typically allow parts of the code to be executed and the intermediate values of variables and other values to be inspected at that point in the code. The IDE might also have functionality to run the code in a mode that writes detailed information about the execution of the code out to a file.

Interpreter and compiler
The detailed differences between an interpreter and a compiler are not very relevant for data analysts. However, the basic difference is that an interpreter executes the code inside a specific environment, such as the IDE, while a compiler runs it outside an environment.

These features allow the analyst to execute the code and obtain the results of the analysis. The compiler is needed to convert the code into a program that can run on computers that do not have an IDE in the programming language used.

Visualisation packages

Visualisation packages are usually referred to as an interface that can display data in a graphical format, such as graphs, maps, animations and so on. However, analysts should not forget that some types of use still require values for these to be given in a tabular format, such as a spreadsheet. Most of the popular types of visualisation package can also present the data in such tabular formats – often in addition to graphical formats.

Popular visualisation packages include Tableau, Qlikview and the Plotly library.

Interactive aggregations

The packages produced by the vendors mentioned above allow easy interaction by end users. When data analysts have created and calculated data extracts in the appropriate format, these users can often change the filters applied to the data in order to view details on specific regions, products and so on. These packages often have features to allow the end users to choose aggregation levels, to change from a count, a sum, an average and so on.

Graphical displays

The main reason for using visualisation packages is normally to allow end users to see graphical summaries of data analysis. This can be in the form of a chart with various colours showing the numbers. It can also be in the form of geographical maps showing the location of customers, or with regions coloured according to population/customer density. Some advanced packages can produce animations where lines or points on graphs move according to the time of the events.

METHODS

A data analyst needs to be familiar with a wide range of techniques to deal with the different stages of the analysis process and the different types of data that are used. Mastery of all the techniques by individual analysts is rarely possible and data analysis projects are often carried out by teams of specialists. However, effective data analysts will need to have a high level of proficiency in at least one of these skills and strong knowledge of the others.

> **TYPES OF DATA**
>
> There are many different groupings of data that can be used for data analysis; common labels include transactional, meta, master and reference data.

Transactional data
The data that is normally processed and stored by operational systems is transactional data. This data is typically recorded once for each interaction on the system and there is often some duplication between each record. For example, this could be that the system records information about the delivery address for each purchase that the customer makes.

The analyst might need to group this information and report the total value of all sales that have gone to the same postal address or region.

Metadata
Metadata is data about data. This might be information such as how many transactions have been processed in a day, or how many records there are in the transaction table. It could also be a library entry for a book describing author, title, publisher and so on.

An analyst will need to ensure that the metadata entries correspond to the data entries that they describe.

Master data
When many operational systems in an organisation contain the same information, there can be duplication of data and conflict between them. For example, this can happen when both the sales system and the marketing system contain information describing the customers. If a customer is recorded as 'C Smith' in the sales system and 'Edward C Smith' in the marketing system, it will have to be decided which one will be used to ensure consistency.

This can be resolved by appointing one of the systems as the master system, whose data ('master data') is to be used and, if possible, copied to all other systems.

> ### Reference data
> Reference data is used to provide restrictions for valid data entries or to provide conversions. For instance, valid data entries can be used to describe country codes and names, to ensure that entries are only chosen from this range. Conversions could be used to describe conversion between units of measurements, such as between metres and feet and inches.
>
> An analyst can use the restrictions that the first type of reference data provides to check that entries are valid and to translate between codes, such as changing a country code to a name. They can use conversion reference tables to harmonise a system that records data in different units.

Data manipulation

The manipulation of data to solve a business problem is the activity that data analysts spend most time doing. It is often said that at least 80 per cent of an analyst's time is spent on this activity. It is usually the first activity undertaken in a new project, as it is required for any subsequent modelling, statistical analysis, machine learning application or presentation of the information found in the data to the stakeholders concerned.

Although they are often associated with data warehousing, all data manipulation activities can be thought of as a set of three categories of activities known under the acronym ETL: extraction, transformation and loading.

> **WHAT IS DATA WAREHOUSING?**
>
> Bill Inmon has defined a data warehouse as 'a subject-oriented, integrated, time-variant and non-volatile collection of data in support of management's decision making process' (Inmon 2005). His approach was focused

> on more rigid architectures, whereas an approach by Ralph Kimball was on pragmatically building dimensional data marts (see the box later in this chapter on star and snowflake schemas). Although there is some tension between these approaches, there have been successful attempts at getting the best from each by combining them.

Data can be manipulated with many different programming languages and on a variety of platforms, from large database systems to small local laptops, but the techniques used on all these systems are similar, although the forms might be different.

Data manipulation alone does not reveal any information, but it is essential in transforming the data into a form that is better suited for analysis.

Extraction

Data often has to be taken from a variety of source systems, which keep data in different formats, encodings and internal models. Either a connection will need to be made to these systems to extract the information required, or the systems will need to store the information in a common format.

It is common for relational database systems to provide a connection with the Open Database Connectivity (ODBC) protocol that can serve as a bridge to many other systems and programming languages. For non-relational databases, other protocols exist that can extract information in Extensible Markup Language (XML) or JavaScript Object Notation (JSON) formats, which are a more general-purpose means of encoding data.

Converting data to a common format solves differences such as those that arise when systems from different geographical regions use different ways of representing characters in languages specific to each region; and those that exist when individual operating systems store and encode the data they hold.

Consider this example: an extract from a source system might be required as a snapshot of the relevant data values; or could be required as an initial snapshot, with subsequent extracts of only updated and new values. If the updated and new values have to be integrated with an initial snapshot, further manipulation is likely to be needed in order for the data to be amenable to analysis.

Transformation

Data transformation is the activity of changing the structure of data so that it is easier to analyse. It can cover both cleaning and reformatting of the data, and there is considerable overlap between the two activities. These two activities are often done repeatedly to get the data into a better state for analysis to be done.

Cleaning data   Cleaning can improve the overall quality as it relates to data analysis, but if it is over-applied or done badly it can reduce the value of analytical results. If data is not cleaned, analysis could result in inaccurate results, which may lead stakeholders to lose trust in the analysis and also result in poor business decisions and damaged business profits.

There are many ways in which data can be 'dirty' and need cleaning:

- **duplicate data:** for example, one customer having several entries;
- **inconsistent data:** for example, the address and postal code not matching;
- **missing data:** for example, missing values;
- **misuse of fields:** for example, recoding the phone number in the address field;
- **incorrect data:** for example, an address that does not exist;
- **inconsistent values:** for example, using different country descriptions, such as UK versus United Kingdom;
- **typing mistakes:** for example, an address that is mistyped.

TOOLS, METHODS AND TECHNIQUES

Reformatting data It is often necessary to use a number of transformations to get data into a format that can be analysed. This problem often stems from the range of different ways data source systems have been designed, with each designed so that it is optimally suited for the purpose it is meant to serve. This can cause difficulties for data analysts trying to analyse data across a broad range of sources.

There can be differences between how the system designers have decided to model the data that their systems hold. An example of this could be a marketing system holding just one record per household, with the occupants identified only as 'A & B Smith', whereas the sales system holds two records of 'Mr Smith' and 'Mrs Smith'. In this instance, the data analyst might have difficulties identifying which individual customer reacted to a marketing campaign, and would therefore have to decide to only report which household has reacted rather than which individual.

There can also be differences between how each of the systems records the same information. A system that covers multiple countries may have a free text field for capturing the address, but a system that deals only with one country may have a strict template for entering road, town and postal code in the correct format. Comparing data between the two types can be challenging, and deciding which one to use can affect the accuracy of the analysis.

In data warehousing, the transformation of data is concerned with modelling the data in a form that can be used for presenting it for further analysis. This might involve normalising the data and converting it into a common schema, and might also include building a star or snowflake model (see Figure 3.6) so that users can extract data using an online analytical processing (OLAP) cube tool, which is purpose-built for such tasks.

If the transformation is done merely to enable data to be useful for a specific analytical purpose, some of these activities can be avoided, but the data will still need to be presented in a suitable format, ready for analysis. This often needs to be a tabular format with rows as individual observations and columns as the attributes of each observation.

Loading

Once data has been extracted, cleaned and transformed, it will then need to be transferred to a system where analysis or visualisation of it can be done. Some of the same problems that are faced in the extraction phase can equally apply to the transference. For example, the data will either need to be directly transferred using a common protocol or exported into a text file that can be read by the statistical system in use.

Statistical analysis

Statistical data analysis methods use mathematical techniques to extract insights hidden in data. This involves building mathematical expressions that approximate the data and uses these expressions to generate predictions.

Statistical techniques can be broadly characterised as descriptive or predictive. Each of these statistical themes is a very broad topic and a full exploration is outside the scope of this book; in this section we will merely introduce them as they relate to data analysis.

Bias

Statistical techniques assume that the data to be analysed is a representative sample of all the values that could be generated from the process they are taken from. For the insight and predictions generated from statistical methods to be valid, it is important to ensure that the data is free from any significant bias.

There are many types of bias that originate from the collection and manipulation of data:

- **Selection bias:** this happens when data is gathered in such a way that it is no longer truly representative of the population. An example of this is when young people are more likely to respond to a survey than older people.

- **Reporting bias:** this occurs if people are more likely to report certain events, such as types of crimes, than other events.

- **Sampling bias:** if more data is available than the computing hardware can handle, it might be necessary to take a subsample, but this sample should be representative of the whole and not merely observations that are first in the data set.

Descriptive analytics

Descriptive analytics is also known as summary statistics, and these techniques are used to deduce key information about a data set. They use existing data about past or known events to describe the process that generated the data. They include both simple techniques on just one variable, and more complex techniques on the interactions of several variables.

> **WHAT IS A VARIABLE?**
>
> A variable is one piece of data about a subject. For example, a subject could be a person and we could record their name, age and gender, which would be three separate variables.

Examples of simple techniques on a single variable are:

- **Count:** the total number of data points.
- **Sum:** the total combined value of all data points.
- **Maximum:** the largest value in the data points.
- **Minimum:** the smallest value in the data points.
- **Range:** the maximum and minimum values.
- **Mean:** the average value of all data points.
- **Median:** the middle value all data points.
- **Mode:** the value that appears most often among the data points.
- **Variance:** a value that describes the distribution of the data points.

DATA ANALYST

A couple of the more complex descriptive analytics techniques on the interaction between several variables are discussed in the following subsections.

Correlation

The interaction between two variables is described by the correlation between them, and can be expressed by several different statistical measures. If the high values of one variable are often seen together with either high or low values of another variable, then the variables are said to be highly correlated. Although there are many different statistical measures to express the strength of this relationship, the one known as the Pearson coefficient, which is represented by the Greek letter rho (ρ), is the most commonly used and is illustrated in Figure 3.2.[1]

Figure 3.2 Examples of correlations in different data sets

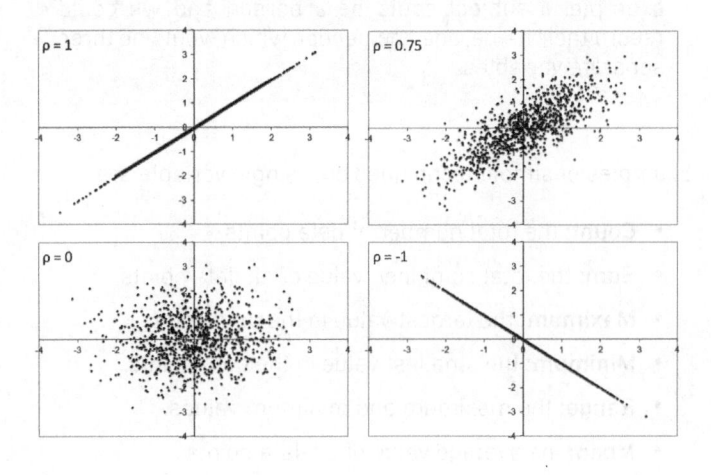

---

1 For more information on the Pearson coefficient, read an introduction here: www.spss-tutorials.com/pearson-correlation-coefficient/

When two variables have a big positive and a big negative number for the Pearson correlation coefficient, between them they are deemed to be highly correlated because the relationship between them is strong.

Significance There are several statistical techniques that can quantify how likely it is to observe a relationship between two variables. It is normally considered significantly interesting and surprising when the observed relationship only has a 1 in 20, or 5 per cent, chance of being randomly generated. This value is normally known as the p-value and the lower this value, the more significant the result is considered.

If repeatedly rolling, say, four fair dice, it will eventually be observed that all four of them lands on a six. Even though it is an unlikely outcome, the large number of experiments (for example, each roll of the dice) will ensure that the outcome is observed and the p-value is large.

With modern computer systems it is possible to analyse many thousands of variables automatically, but when doing so it is almost inevitable that some of them have interesting or surprising relationships. It is important to understand that this might not necessarily be a feature of the variables, but could be merely a feature of the enormous number of automatic tests that the computers are doing.

Predictive analytics

Predictive analytics is used to calculate the expected values of a variable for observations that we have not seen in the data. For example, if we know that one apple costs £1, two apples costs £1.50 and three apples costs £2, then we might propose that apples cost 50p each, plus 50p – and therefore predict that four apples would cost £2.50. Existing or past observations are used to make a generalisation of the process that generates the data, and this is used to predict new values.

Regression An alternative way to represent the relationship between two variables is regression analysis. This technique can be used to describe the relationship between more than two variables where one of the variables is considered dependent on, or predicted by, the other variables. The variable that is predicted is called the dependent variable and the other variables are called independent variables. The mathematics of this model assumes that all the independent variables are uncorrelated, and the correlation technique described earlier in this chapter can be used to verify this condition.

There are a number of models of how the relationship between variables can be represented, and these are known as general linear models. The simplest of these is the linear regression model, where the dependent variable is related to the linear combination of the parameters for the independent variables. The calculation of the regression model is concerned with finding these constant parameters and analysing how well they fit the data.

Often, the data for the dependent and the independent variables needs to be transformed to conform to the requirements for the model and, in this situation, the analyst will need to go back to data manipulation tasks.

When the regression model has been built it can be used to describe what change there would be in the dependent variable given a change in *one* of the independent variables and assuming all other variables stay the same. This can give the data analyst a good indication of what overall effect each of the independent variables has and the strength of this relationship. It can also be used to predict what values the dependent variable will take in situations that have not been seen in the input data – such as what values it might take in future situations.

Interpolation and extrapolation Many of the statistical models that represent the relationship between different variables, such as the regression models just described, can also be used to predict what values the predicted variable would take when the independent variables take new values. When the model is used to predict new outcomes that are within the range of values for the independent variable it is called interpolation, and when it is used to predict outcomes for input values outside the range of existing values it is called extrapolation (see Figure 3.3).

The distinction between these two types of prediction is important: outcomes that are outside the range of the existing data points are more uncertain, because we have not seen how the process that generates this data behaves in these circumstances.

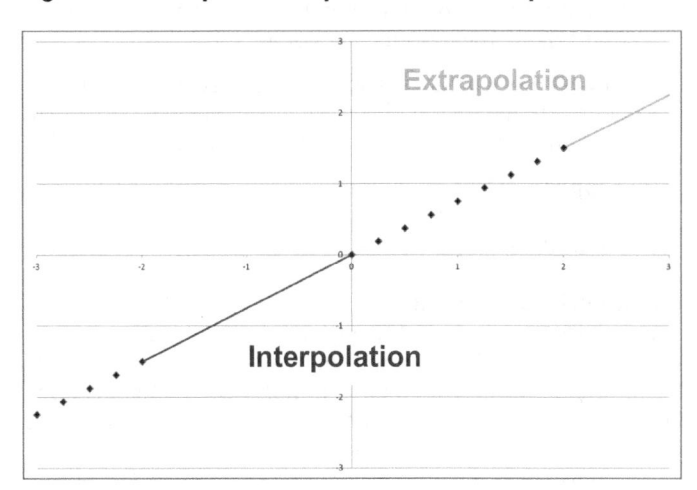

Figure 3.3 Example of interpolation and extrapolation

Machine learning

Machine learning uses techniques inspired by the way that natural and biological processes react to inputs and adapt to their environment. It involves the building of algorithms capable of making predictions or generalisations directly from input data, without reference to the processes that generate the data.

These techniques can be grouped into two types of algorithms: supervised learning and unsupervised learning.

Supervised learning

In supervised learning, the relationship between input variables and output variables is examined and the outcome can be used to predict likely values for the output, given new values for the input. Many of these techniques do not have the same strict restrictions on the characteristics of the input variables as traditional statistical regression has for its dependent variables. Examples of supervised learning techniques are:

- **Genetic algorithms:** these are inspired by genetic evolution and Darwin's 'survival of the fittest' hypothesis to find the best possible combination of input parameters that give high values for the output.
- **Neural networks:** these are inspired by the neural connections in the brain and can be used to make systems that are able to adapt to changes in the inputs.
- **Support vector machines:** this is a popular type of clustering algorithm that can be used as an alternative to the traditional generalised linear regression techniques.

Unsupervised learning

In unsupervised learning, the algorithm is not given an output variable as a target, but only a set of inputs from which it will try to find patterns. The most common type of unsupervised learning is clustering algorithms, which will attempt to group the input observations together in collections that share the same characteristics or are closely related to each other. Of these, the most common and popular type of unsupervised learning algorithms is K-means clustering (Trevino 2016). This has the benefit of being relatively easy to implement on parallel computing platforms and can therefore perform very well on large data sets.

Data visualisation

Visualisation methods make it easier for humans to see patterns in complicated data, and they are also used to communicate the results from traditional statistical or modern machine learning techniques. This approach is focused on how human decision-makers need to have analytical results presented in order to understand them efficiently.

Traditionally, Microsoft Excel has been very extensively used for graphical representations of data, but more advanced data analysis tools, such as R and Python, are becoming common. Both of these languages contain a large range of freely available modules that are able to create very advanced visualisations of data. This includes interactive visualisations in which a programmer develops template web pages which the end user can filter, zoom and rescale to fit their needs. Examples of these modules include matplotlib, seaborn and bokeh for Python and ggplot2 and Plotly for R.

TECHNIQUES

Successful data analysis requires many different techniques. Most of these techniques have been around for decades, but they are being refined for use in our modern Big Data environment. Each technique has strengths and weaknesses, which makes them suitable for specific types of problem.

Programming

Programming languages are used to manipulate data and there are many different variants available; some are designed as general-purpose languages, and some are intended to deal with specific types of problem.

Programming techniques
This section will introduce a number of popular programming techniques and some of the languages in common use in data analysis.

Imperative programming Imperative programming is the most common and widely used technique, both within the data analysis community and in the wider IT development community. This is the technique that most people associate with programming and is often the first style of programming taught in beginner level courses. It owes its popularity to its wide range of powerful applications and its relative ease of use.

In this style of programming, there are three fundamental concepts:

- **Sequencing:** the program will be executed line by line from top to bottom.
- **Selection:** statements are written in the code that select which lines of code to execute and which to omit, based on a given condition. The most common is the IF statement.
- **Iteration:** these are statements that will execute the same code repeatedly until a condition is met. This is achieved with 'for' loops or 'while' loops.

WHAT IS AN IF STATEMENT?

The most common form of selection or conditional logic is the IF statement, which must be written slightly differently in different programming languages. However, the common elements are the same: a condition that is either true or false and two separate blocks of code, A and B. The IF statement will execute only block A if the condition is true, and only block B if the condition is false. In some programming languages, block B can be missing, in which case the code in block A is skipped if the condition is false.

WHAT IS A LOOP?

Doing the same task many times is called iteration and is one of the major advantages of using computers – they can rapidly repeat a task many, many times. The most common and simplest form of iteration is a 'for' loop that usually consists of a variable, a list of values that it should take and a block of code. The block of code will then be repeatedly executed with the variable taking each of the values in the list.

Declarative programming One of the alternatives to imperative programming is the declarative style, where the code will not specify how to achieve the desired outcome, but only what that outcome is.

To delete all the odd numbers from a list, for instance, an imperative program will need to specify the iteration of the list and the selection of the odd numbers, which are then deleted. In the declarative style, the program will merely have to specify the delete operation and the condition for the odd numbers. As can be seen in Figure 3.4, this can lead to very concisely written code.

Figure 3.4 Examples of imperative and declarative code

Imperative style	Declarative style

numbers = [1,2,3,4,5,6,7,8,9]
for i in numbers:
  if int(i%2) == 0:
    numbers.remove(i)
	numbers = [1,2,3,4,5,6,7,8,9]
	numbers = list(filter(lambda i: i%2!= 0, numbers))

One very popular example of declarative programming is SQL mentioned earlier. In this language, the actual operations taken to compute the same SELECT statement could be different on systems that are not from the same producer.

Functional programming Using the functional programming approach, the computations never change the data, but create and store new data as a result of manipulations. This approach is inspired by the way mathematical functions operate when there are well-defined input parameters and output data and has its origins in the field of lambda calculus.

Because of its foundations in mathematical theory and extensive research connected to proving the correctness of functions, functional programming is gaining popularity among programmers. This is also because it provides much simpler and easier ways of converting code into parallel execution programs.

Modularisation Procedural languages enable the definition of separate sections of code that achieve specific purposes. A section could be a segment of code used multiple times or used by multiple programs. These individual sections of code are modules that provide specific functionality and they can each build on the functionality of other modules to enable advanced behaviour.

The pre-supplied functions that come with these languages are examples of modules that achieve such specified functionality. They provide well-defined ways to perform simple manipulations of data and are used by programmers to build more complex functionality. Many languages come with a wide library of such modules that have been built by other teams of developers. These teams often make their modules freely available to the community of programmers that use this language. This provides individual programmers with new ways to perform complex data manipulations.

It is also possible for individual programmers and analysts to separate out modules that need to be used multiple times in the same code, or need to be used by multiple pieces of code. These modules could be ones that make a specific calculation used in the organisation or transformation needed for the organisation's types of information.

When designing and building such modules, it is important to remember the following concepts:

- **Coupling**: this is the interdependency between different modules in a system and measures the relationship between modules.
- **Cohesion**: this is the degree to which the elements inside a module belong together and measures the relationship within modules.

Good software that is well structured and is easy to maintain has a low coupling (relationship between modules) with a high cohesion (relationship within modules). Low coupling often also leads to low cohesion and vice versa, so practical software design is concerned with achieving the best balance between the two.

SQL – the database query language

One of the most popular programming languages for data analysts is SQL. It is a specialist language designed to deal with manipulation of data stored in a RDBMS. It has been an international standard since the late 1980s and has since undergone several reviews and extensions that have expanded the functionality of the language. It is an example of a declarative language.

SQL defines a number of commands that the analyst can use to modify data or change a database in various ways. This includes simple techniques to extract and manipulate data and also advanced optimisation methods and techniques to build applications that use the database to provide other functionalities, such as triggering automatic code to run when certain conditions are met, code that reverses effects when an error has occurred, user defined functions, and many more. Many of these features are not essential for data analysis, however.

A full overview of the extensive abilities of SQL is outside the scope of this book, so this section will merely provide a very short introduction to one part that is essential for data analysts. There are many websites and books which provide more comprehensive coverage of SQL.

SELECT statement The most popular SQL command for data analysts is the SELECT statement, which is used to define a new table with information derived from the existing tables contained in a database. A typical use of this statement is to define a table that is extracted for further processing inside or outside the database.

The SQL SELECT statement consists of a number of clauses that describe what the resulting table should contain. The most important clauses are:

- The SELECT clause, which describes what columns should be contained in the output.
- The FROM clause, which describes which existing tables the data should come from and how they should be joined together.
- The WHERE clause, which describes how to filter the rows in the resulting data set.
- The GROUP BY clause, which describes any grouping of columns and work in connection with aggregate functions described in the SELECT clause.
- The ORDER BY clause, which describes any ordering that has to be applied.

EXAMPLE SQL SELECT STATEMENT

```
SELECT department.name AS department_name,
       SUM(employee.salary) AS total_salary
FROM employee
JOIN department
       ON employee.dept_cd = department.dept_cd
WHERE employee.start_date >= '2016-01-01'
GROUP BY department.name
ORDER BY department.name;
```

The powerful syntax of the SELECT statement enables analysts to perform a range of advanced data manipulation tasks. The most common tasks are:

- Restricting the rows in the resulting data set, which can be done with the SELECT clause. This clause also has to specify the aggregate functions to be applied to the groups of rows that are defined in the GROUP BY clause.
- Searching for records that fulfil certain criteria, which is achieved by using the WHERE clause to filter the

records on that criteria. These criteria can range from a simple value in a single column or it can be a complex combination of several columns from multiple linked tables.

- Grouping of the records, which can be done with the use of the GROUP BY clause and aggregate functions in the SELECT clause. There are a large range of aggregate functions to provide a sum, mean, count of values, standard deviation and many more.
- Sorting the records, which can be done by using the ORDER BY clause, and enables subsequent external analysis to process each row in the resulting table in a given order.

In SQL there are also many auxiliary functions that can be used to manipulate individual data values, such as functions to get the absolute value of a number, to get the difference between two dates, to get the upper case of a string and so on.

Advanced query techniques There are many techniques enabling data analysts to write efficient queries that extract data from relational database systems. Comprehensive coverage of these is outside the scope of this book; however, the extraction of information from databases is a crucial skill for data analysts and this section will provide a short introduction to one of the most common techniques.

Query daisy chains: The SELECT statement can be used to extract data from a database for use by other external software, but it can also be used to create new tables that can be stored within the database. This is done by adding a create table clause at the beginning of the statement.

SQL CREATE TABLE STATEMENT EXAMPLE

CREATE TABLE department_total_salaries AS
SELECT department.name AS department_name,
    SUM(employee.salary) AS total_salary

```
FROM employee
JOIN department
      ON employee.dept_cd = department.dept_cd
WHERE employee.start_date >= '2016-01-01'
GROUP BY department.name
ORDER BY department.name;
```

This enables the analyst to use the newly created table in subsequent queries. By using this method sequentially, the analyst can chain the statements together so that each created table is subsequently used to create yet new tables. This technique is essentially daisy chains of queries and can result in complicated code that creates many intermediary tables before arriving at the final table.

An alternative to creating a table is to use the SELECT statement to define a view that is exactly like a table but does not contain any data; this can make subsequent queries perform much faster. This is done be using 'CREATE VIEW <view_name> AS' in the above code. A view can be used in any place where a table would be used, and when the database management system sees that a view is used it will calculate its data before continuing with the other code.

Python
The Python language and its associated development environment is becoming very popular among data analysts as it is a powerful language that is free to use and easy to learn. It is an example of a general-purpose language and can be used with a variety of programming styles.

The language consists of a core set of commands which can be extended by downloading packages from a very comprehensive, and free, online repository.[2] This repository has packages that enable the programmer to do a wide

---

2   See https://pypi.org/project/pip/

variety of tasks, from working with structured data sets to implementing machine learning algorithms.

Proprietary languages

There exist a number of languages that are used exclusively with particular vendor tools. The best known of these are the languages developed by SPSS, SAS and Matlab. These are suppliers of some of the most popular tools for general data manipulation and statistical calculations. Other popular proprietary languages are described below.

Excel and VBA   The syntax used for advanced computations in Microsoft Excel and its companion programming language, VBA, can be used for data manipulation and statistical calculations. Although good for rudimentary data manipulations, they are widely considered to be too limited for more advanced computations where more powerful languages are needed.

Hadoop languages   The Apache Hadoop system is a free and open-source system for storing and manipulating massive data sets. It works by combining many smaller computers into a cooperating system where each calculates a small subset of the problem before the results are combined to give the end result.

This system uses a set of specialist programming techniques that are specifically aimed at handling the distributed calculations. It uses the general-purpose Java language to implement the MapReduce programming model, which is a functional programming technique. The Hadoop system also provides limited support for SQL.

Testing

An important part of ensuring that developed code is correct and free from errors is the process of testing the code. Three important types of testing are:

- **Unit testing:** when using the modularisation technique described earlier in this chapter, it is possible to test each module individually to ascertain that it fulfils its specification. This involves executing the module with a range of parameters and comparing these to the expected outcomes.

- **Integration testing:** when several modules have been independently developed, it is important to test whether they are able to work together to achieve their combined purpose.
- **Regression testing:** software is changed for a variety of reasons, such as to improve its speed or to expand its functionality. When completing such a change, it is important not just to test that the new aim has been reached but also to ensure that the old functionality has been maintained.

Data modelling and business analysis

Business analysis is the process of identifying the requirements to solve a business need and designing a solution that will satisfy these requirements. The purpose of data modelling is to organise business data into entities and to describe their properties and relationships. Data analysts are often involved in both of these activities, as well as implementing the agreed solution. This is important in order to gain knowledge of the business context of the data and thereby understand the processes that generate that data. It is these processes that the analysis will describe and ultimately change, so it is crucial that data analysts are knowledgeable about them.

Data is a central aspect of most organisations today, and identifying business requirements often involves analysing relevant data about the business problem. This is a central task that involves understanding the business processes, gathering relevant data and extracting information from this data.

Understanding and mapping business processes is a large and complex subject outside the scope of this book. This section will mainly deal with the associated subject of mapping data relationships and data flows.

It is important that data analysts are able to both read and understand such models to be able to effectively extract information from the systems they describe. It is often the case that such models are not available, correct or complete, and so data analysts might need to build data models from scratch.

Relational models

When modelling data in the relational model, data is organised according to the entities that it belongs to. Entities represent anything for which information can be recorded: a physical object, such as a car or person, or an abstract concept such as an organisation or event. The items of information that are recorded for each entity are called attributes and the associations between them are called relations.

Entity-relationship diagrams When modelling data for relational models, it typical to represent these models in entity-relationship diagrams (ER diagrams, see Figure 3.5). These diagrams can be used to develop a model gradually so that it can be implemented in a RDBMS. There are three traditional types of models used:

- **Conceptual model:** this focuses on the business representation of the entities from business analysis, but does not yet consider the database considerations for implementation.
- **Logical model:** this builds on the conceptual model and considers the storage types for the attributes, but does not yet represent an implementable solution.
- **Physical model:** this refines the logical model so that it is capable of being implemented in a RDBMS.

In a fully developed model, each entry is typically represented by a separate table and its attributes are the columns in the table.

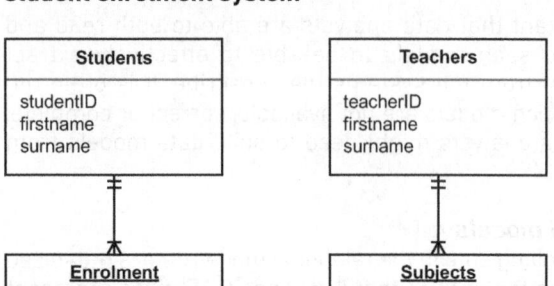

Figure 3.5 Example ER diagram showing a simplified student enrolment system

```
┌─────────────────┐              ┌─────────────────┐
│    Students     │              │    Teachers     │
├─────────────────┤              ├─────────────────┤
│ studentID       │              │ teacherID       │
│ firstname       │              │ firstname       │
│ surname         │              │ surname         │
└────────┬────────┘              └────────┬────────┘
         │                                │
┌────────┴────────┐              ┌────────┴────────┐
│   Enrolment     │              │    Subjects     │
├─────────────────┤              ├─────────────────┤
│ studentID       ├──────────────┤ subjectID       │
│ subjectID       │              │ teacherID       │
│                 │              │ subjectTitle    │
└─────────────────┘              └─────────────────┘
```

The data about student entities would be stored in a student table, for instance, where each row represents a student. The columns of the table would represent all the attributes of each student and there would be columns used to link it with entities represented by other tables; for example, a column with an identification code can be used to link to the subjects that the student has enrolled in.

Normalisation One of the advantages of the relational model is that it is capable of storing data in a way that ensures the integrity of the data. Duplication of information in the system, such as when an employee's salary is recorded in the employee table and the total department salary is recorded in the department table, can lead to errors if the information in one place is updated, inserted or deleted but not in the other.

In relational databases it is very common to use the process of normalisation to eliminate such duplication, which can ensure better organisation, integrity and flexibility of the database. This happens through a process by which the data structures are manipulated into a form where these anomalies are not possible. It is common to talk about data that is structured in unnormalised, 1st, 2nd and 3rd normal form, which gradually reduces the number of anomalies that can occur. Each of these forms is clearly defined and there are even some that define higher forms for specific circumstances.

Data warehouse models

Database systems used to support operational business systems, such as web sales systems, are not very good at supporting analytics. It is important that they are always available and can respond quickly to requests from the users, which usually only involve a small number of records. They are also typically organised in a relational model and normalised to ensure their integrity. In contrast, analytical requests typically involve a large number of records in a batch and, since the data is updated only once a day, the integrity of it becomes less of a concern.

This difference has led to the development of data warehouse systems that read data from the operational systems overnight, when they are not busy, and can be organised to serve the organisation's analytical needs. The main concern for analytical users is to ensure that data coming from different systems is presented in the same format; for example, in one system a sale might have transaction code 2, while in another it might be transaction code 'TRN'.

Three-layer architecture It is very common in data warehouses to have a three-layer architecture comprising the following:

- **Staging:** the intermediate storage area that the data is saved to when extracted from the source systems. This is typically only the data that has been generated since the last update.

- **Detailed:** this layer consolidates the data from the staging layer tables from different source systems.

- **Mart:** this layer presents the data for relevant reporting purposes. It is common to have a sales mart and a customer mart that both contain individual customer details; however, one of them will only have one row per customer while the other has multiple rows.

Kimball dimensional modelling An alternative to data marts that was developed by Ralph Kimball and called 'dimensional modelling' (Kimball and Ross 2013). In this type of model there is one or more fact table, containing one row per object/event being reported, that has a number of defined dimensions.

The customer address could be such a dimension, with a number of levels such as country, town and street. This enables the development of reporting systems known as OLAP cubes to present the total sales by country, and the user can then 'drill down' to individual towns, streets or house numbers.

A popular method of logically organising systems that have been modelled in this way is to create a star or snowflake schema, as shown in Figure 3.6.

> **WHAT ARE STAR AND SNOWFLAKE SCHEMAS?**
>
> The star and snowflake schema model for data marts was developed and promoted by Ralph Kimball. The star schema is a simplified and more commonly used version of a snowflake schema where there is only one layer of dimension tables around the fact table (see Figure 3.6). When there are dimension tables around the dimension tables it becomes a snowflake schema.

Object-oriented modelling

In object-oriented modelling, data is organised into a system of interacting objects. It is a model that is used very extensively in software development, and many modern programming languages are organised according to this model. The focus of this approach is the behaviour of each object and particularly how this behaviour is achieved by the collaboration between objects.

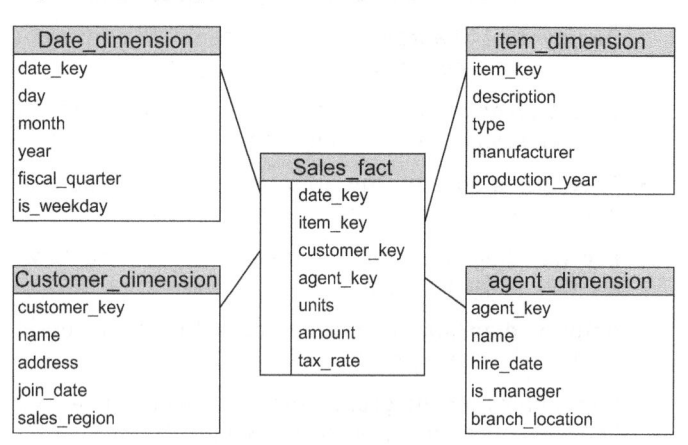

Figure 3.6 Example of a star schema

Date_dimension
date_key
day
month
year
fiscal_quarter
is_weekday

Sales_fact
date_key
item_key
customer_key
agent_key
units
amount
tax_rate

item_dimension
item_key
description
type
manufacturer
production_year

Customer_dimension
customer_key
name
address
join_date
sales_region

agent_dimension
agent_key
name
hire_date
is_manager
branch_location

In this model, each object owns its own data, which includes the relationship it holds with other objects. Its behaviour is defined by its public interface, which includes all the commands that it will respond to – also known as functions. Each object can be grouped into collections that will respond to the same commands. For example, a car and a lorry will both be in the group 'Vehicle' and therefore respond to the command 'Drive' – although they each might do so in different ways.

Unified Modelling Language diagrams Unified Modelling Language (UML) is a modelling language developed to provide a standard for visual representations of the models used in software engineering. The representations are very commonly used for business analysis and object-oriented models. There are 14 diagrams that can be used to represent the structure, behaviour and interactions between objects:

- **Class diagram:** this represents the static structure of a system.
- **Component diagram:** this represents the structural interdependencies of a system.

- **Composite structure diagram:** this represents the internal structure and collaborations of a system.
- **Deployment diagram:** this represents the physical structural element of a system.
- **Object diagram:** this represents an actual structural state of a system at a point in time.
- **Package diagram:** this represents the structural interdependencies between packages of a system.
- **Profile diagram:** this represents the structural stereotypes of a system.
- **Activity diagram:** this represents the behavioural workflow in a system.
- **Communication diagram:** this represents an actual behavioural communication in a system.
- **Interaction overview diagram:** this represents the behavioural interactions in a system.
- **Sequence diagram:** this represents an actual behavioural sequence of messages in a system.
- **State diagram:** this represents the behavioural states that a system can have.
- **Timing diagram:** this represents the behavioural timing constraints that a system has.
- **Use case diagram:** this represents the behavioural interactions a user can have with a system.

For data analysis, the most important diagrams are the class diagram, which contains the objects with their respective data values, and the use case diagram, which details how users can interact with a system. However, all the diagrams will give important information about a system that is valuable when analysing data.

Change management and project management

Much of the work for data analysts involves projects that change the organisations they are engaged with. Sometimes these projects are done as part of a larger team, and analysts will need to appreciate the contributions of other specialists in the team in order to collaborate effectively with them. Other times, data analysts are not supported by other specialists and will need to undertake some of these responsibilities themselves, such as project management and business change management.

This means that a data analyst needs to be aware of the common project management methods and how they contribute to the success of the change process. There are many project management methods; this section will merely introduce two of the most commonly encountered.

> A data analyst is a bridge between the customer and the business. We rely on analysts to extract meaningful data and produce reports. Analysts need to work in tandem with marketers to generate insights.
> (Kalindini Patel, Senior Global Manager, Smith & Nephew)

PRINCE2

The PRINCE2 project management method was developed by the UK government in the early 1990s as a way to develop IT projects. It has become a de facto standard for projects in the UK public sector and has been implemented outside the IT industry and gained widespread adoption outside the UK.

The acronym stands for PRojects In a Controlled Environment and the method provides a structured and adaptable framework for managing projects. There is comprehensive guidance for adhering to this framework, which includes qualifications for candidates that pass an accredited exam. The guidance includes seven principles, seven themes and seven processes, as well as 26 suggested management products which are the documentation that can be produced by a project (Bennett and AXELOS 2017).

The seven principles of PRINCE2 are:

- **Continued business justification:** it is important that the justification for a project is not just agreed and signed off at the start, but continues to be reviewed throughout the project.
- **Learn from experience:** it is vital for the continued success of projects in an organisation that experience from past projects is recorded and applied to subsequent projects.
- **Defined roles and responsibilities:** in PRINCE2 projects, the roles and responsibilities for managing projects are defined and agreed.
- **Manage by stages:** projects are managed, organised and monitored in defined stages.
- **Manage by exception:** when agreed limits are exceeded or expected to be exceeded, this is immediately escalated to the appropriate authority.
- **Focus on products:** a PRINCE2 project is focused on the delivery and qualities of its products.
- **Tailor to suit the project environment:** the PRINCE2 method used for a particular project should be tailored to suit the organisation and the specific characteristics of the project.

The PRINCE2 method has many proponents, but has also attracted some criticism. Although being described by AXELOS, the owners, as suitable for any size of project, it is sometimes considered too formal and comprehensive for smaller organisations or projects. It is also sometimes criticised for not teaching the training course candidates sufficient techniques to use in projects, such as requirements gathering, stakeholder management, financial project appraisals and so on.

Agile
The Agile software development methodology was developed in the early 2000s as an alternative to the prevailing traditional waterfall methods, most notably the PRINCE2 method, that

were considered too focused on documentation and following a prescribed process. It was created as a way to ensure that software could be rapidly developed with only the required focus on formality.

The signatories to the Agile Manifesto wanted to develop software that followed four values:

- individuals and interactions over processes and tools;
- working software over comprehensive documentation;
- customer collaboration over contract negotiation;
- responding to change over following a plan.

This group of thought leaders also agreed on 12 principles that covered the Agile Alliance. This movement has given rise to a wide variety of techniques and development methods that implement these values and principles.

More information on Agile can be found on the Agile Manifesto website[3] and in Measey et al. (2015).

Time-boxing One of the most prevalent features of Agile projects is the adoption of time-boxing for development phases. As opposed to traditional project management methods, where all the features of the final software are documented and agreed before the development is started, in the time-boxing method a limited set of features is agreed to be developed in the next time-box. When a time-box is nearing completion, the features for the next iteration are agreed. This means that fully functional software is rapidly developed, although with limited functionality, and delivered to the customer. With each iteration of a time-box, the customer gets more and more of the functionality until the project completes. In traditional methods, the project's money or time could run out without a fully functioning system having been developed. The benefit of time-boxing is that even if the requirements for features grow throughout the project, the customer still has functional software.

---

[3] See http://agilemanifesto.org/

SUMMARY

This chapter has introduced the variety of tools, methods and techniques that a data analyst needs to use on a fairly regular basis. These come from the areas of computing and statistics, machine learning, programming, and project and change management disciplines. All these areas can fill several books and courses in their own right. It requires in-depth study and continuous improvement of these skills to master them and progress in a career as data analyst. Career development is discussed in Chapter 5.

A specialist set of skills, methods and techniques that has not been covered in this chapter is the best practice and regulatory knowledge needed to handle sensitive data securely and legally. An introduction to this topic is the subject of the next chapter.

4 RELEVANT REGULATIONS AND BEST PRACTICES FOR DATA ANALYSTS

There are two dimensions to correct practice for data analysts working with data; compliance with legal and regulatory requirements, which forms the first part of this chapter; and giving themselves the best chance for success by looking at data quality and thinking about the data community, which is covered in the second part.

WORKING WITH OTHER PEOPLE'S DATA

Nowadays, businesses are able to link their customer information together with that from third parties, such as social media sites, to create a rich picture of what their customers are motivated by. Some will have this expertise in-house; others will do so supported by specialist marketing agencies or analytics companies.

Many users are unaware that the provision of a service free at the point of consumption, such as Facebook, is funded by the business making use of their data. When this comes to light, the response can be extremely negative – particularly when the service and the use to which it puts data do not have an obvious link.

> **EXAMPLE**
>
> unroll.me is a web service that promises to help users manage large amounts of received marketing emails. Once given access to a user's mailbox, it can create

> a digest email for them – and also make it easy to unsubscribe ('unroll') from these emails.
>
> What users were not aware of was how unroll.me would sell this data on, which only came to public attention through a *New York Times* investigation into Uber.
>
> This report identified that Slice Intelligence (the owners of unroll.me) collected emailed receipts from a rival taxi service called Lyft and sold the information, which was anonymised, to Uber. Uber then used the data as a proxy for the health of Lyft's business.
>
> (www.nytimes.com/2017/04/24/technology/personal-data-firm-slice-unroll-me-backlash-uber.html)

Is this good for us?

Developments in data usage often lead towards increased personalisation; advertising is more targeted to what the user is interested in, and websites may change what they display to prioritise certain offerings. In an area such as insurance, enhanced data and analytics may enable more personalised pricing, so those with healthier lifestyles or who drive more carefully may get cheaper cover than those who are more sedentary or drive more erratically.

But where there are winners, there are also losers. Do we want a world where it is impossible to find insurance because you are considered a high risk? Do you want to find that airline tickets cost more because the airline thinks that you are richer than another customer? Indeed, a travel service, orbitz.com, experimented with showing more expensive hotel rooms to those using Apple devices, reasoning that Apple users have more expensive tastes than PC users.[1]

---

1   See https://business.time.com/2012/06/26/orbitz-shows-higher-prices-to-mac-users/

In October 2017 *Wired* magazine published an article by Rachel Botsman (2017b) – an extract from her book (2017a) – describing a Chinese government scheme that analyses data on its citizens, planned to go live in 2020:

> Imagine a world where many of your daily activities were constantly monitored and evaluated: what you buy at the shops and online; where you are at any given time; who your friends are and how you interact with them; how many hours you spend watching content or playing video games; and what bills and taxes you pay (or not).
>
> ... Now imagine a system where all these behaviours are rated as either positive or negative and distilled into a single number, according to rules set by the government. That would create your Citizen Score and it would tell everyone whether or not you were trustworthy. Plus, your rating would be publicly ranked against that of the entire population and used to determine your eligibility for a mortgage or a job, where your children can go to school – or even just your chances of getting a date.

Possibilities such as these have led some governments to step in and create laws around what can and can't be done.

THE REGULATORY RESPONSE

This section reviews the laws and regulations that have been introduced over time to respond to the changing use of data.

Data Protection Act (DPA)

The increasing use of computers in the 1970s first prompted concerns about the risks they posed to privacy. In 1981 the Council of Europe Convention established standards in member countries to ensure the free flow of information among them without infringing personal privacy. This was followed by the UK's Data Protection Acts in 1984 and 1998.

However, these Acts pre-dated the development of the internet, and do not directly address some of the challenges to privacy in the internet age. To give some context: although Amazon.com did operate in 1998, Google only launched in September of that year, and there was no YouTube, no iPhone and no Facebook.

The DPA (1984) introduced the government role of Data Protection Registrar. That role grew over time and, in 2001, became the Information Commissioner's Office (ICO). The ICO describes itself as: 'The UK's independent authority set up to uphold information rights in the public interest, promoting openness by public bodies and data privacy for individuals.'[2]

Privacy and Electronic Communications Regulations (PECR)

The response to the arrival of the internet and email was partially addressed by the PECR in 2003, and later amended in 2004, 2011, 2015 and 2016. PECR gives people specific privacy rights in relation to electronic communications.

There are specific rules on:

- marketing calls, emails, texts and faxes;
- cookies (and similar technologies);
- keeping communications services secure; and
- customer privacy regarding traffic and location data, itemised billing, phone number identification and directory listings.

PECR continues to apply alongside the GDPR.

GENERAL DATA PROTECTION REGULATION (GDPR)

The GDPR was created by the EU to bring the laws on data privacy into the current age. GDPR became law on 25 May

---

[2] See https://ico.org.uk/

2016, with enforcement commencing two years later, on 25 May 2018.

GDPR applies to all EU member states, but also applies to any businesses worldwide doing business in the EU or with an EU customer. It became law before 'Brexit', but in any event, the British government has adopted the GDPR (and, in fact, strengthened it in some respects) as British law – the DPA 2018.[3]

The main responsibilities for organisations come from the six data protection principles, set out in Article 5,[4] which require that personal data shall be:

1. processed lawfully, fairly and in a transparent manner in relation to individuals;
2. collected for specified, explicit and legitimate purposes and not further processed in a manner that is incompatible with those purposes; further processing for archiving purposes in the public interest, scientific or historical research purposes or statistical purposes shall not be considered to be incompatible with the initial purposes;
3. adequate, relevant and limited to what is necessary in relation to the purposes for which they are processed;
4. accurate and, where necessary, kept up to date; every reasonable step must be taken to ensure that personal data that are inaccurate, having regard to the purposes for which they are processed, are erased or rectified without delay;
5. kept in a form which permits identification of data subjects for no longer than is necessary for the purposes for which the personal data are processed; personal data may be stored for longer periods insofar as the personal data will be processed solely for archiving purposes in the

---

[3] See https://ico.org.uk/for-organisations/data-protection-act-2018/

[4] From GDPR, see https://gdpr-info.eu/art-5-gdpr/ and https://eur-lex.europa.eu/eli/reg/2016/679/oj

public interest, scientific or historical research purposes or statistical purposes subject to implementation of the appropriate technical and organisational measures required by the GDPR in order to safeguard the rights and freedoms of individuals;

6. processed in a manner that ensures appropriate security of the personal data, including protection against unauthorised or unlawful processing and against accidental loss, destruction or damage, using appropriate technical or organisational measures.

In the next section, we'll explain some of the terms and principles in the GDPR, and how they affect data analysts.

Understanding the GDPR

GDPR only applies to personal data so, before we go further, let's consider what that means.

Data classification

Looking after data incurs costs. These can relate to activities such as its storage, archive, backup, encryption, monitoring, profiling and cleansing.

As data volumes increase, and these costs rise, it makes sense to only do these activities on data that requires it. It may be easy to say that 'all of the files on the corporate network belonging to Finance should be encrypted and backed up offsite', but is it sensible to do this for the spreadsheet of the team tea rota; or the 'secret Santa'?

The solution comes in the form of data classification. Three standard levels are:

- **Public:** there is no restriction on sharing this data, such as financial figures in the published annual accounts that are freely available to anyone.
- **Confidential:** data that the organisation doesn't want to share, but it wouldn't be the end of the world if it happened, such as footfall in different stores for a retailer.

RELEVANT REGULATIONS AND BEST PRACTICES FOR DATA ANALYSTS

- **Highly confidential:** data that would have a significant adverse effect on the organisation if it became public, such as details of profit margins or employee salaries.

GDPR leads us to data classifications for personal data, specifically **personal data** and **sensitive personal data.**

> **NOTE**
>
> Some texts will refer to personally identifiable information (PII). PII is a term more commonly used in North America, and covers data items that could be used to identify an individual, such as name, address and birth date. Personal data, as defined by the GDPR, has a broader scope, including data such as postings on social media and Internet Protocol (IP) addresses.
>
> PII data is personal data; but not all personal data is PII.
>
> However, be aware that this distinction is not widely observed, and your organisation may be using the terms interchangeably. If in doubt, ask!

Personal data
The ICO website states:[5]

> Personal data only includes information relating to natural persons who:
>
> - can be identified or who are identifiable directly from the information in question; or
> - who can be indirectly identified from that information in combination with other information.

---

5 See https://ico.org.uk/for-organisations/guide-to-the-general-data-protection-regulation-gdpr/key-definitions/what-is-personal-data/

There is no complete list of types of personal data – much depends on context and what other data is available. There are also some data items, such as name, address and phone number, which may not be personal data in some cases, but will usually be treated as personal data universally. Examples: David Smith is not a unique name; a house may have multiple tenants; and a family home with a landline phone links one phone number to multiple people. Examples of personal data might be:

- name;
- address;
- gender;
- marital status;
- contact details (for example, phone numbers);
- email address;
- national insurance number (or local equivalent in other countries);
- date of birth;
- bank account details;
- credit card details;
- job title;
- images, video or voice recordings (for example, phone calls or CCTV footage);
- cookies and IP addresses.

Although the above data types can be considered as personal data, there are simple changes that can render it non-personal.

- Instead of a specific date of birth, store and use the month and year.
- Instead of a full address, store and the use the first part of the postcode.

What other simple changes can you come up with?

Sensitive personal data
Although sensitive personal data is harder to look after, it's easier to define! The GDPR sets it out in Article 9:[6]

1. racial or ethnic origin;
2. political opinions;
3. religious or philosophical beliefs;
4. trade union membership;
5. genetic data;
6. biometric data;
7. data concerning health (both physical and mental health are included);
8. data concerning a natural person's sex life or sexual orientation.

Why might you, as an individual, be more concerned about these types of information than other information about you?

Elements of GDPR relevant to the data analyst

The full text of the GDPR drives activity across many parts of an organisation, so in this section, we'll pick out elements relevant to the data analyst and their role.

Principle 1 – Lawfulness, fairness and transparency
This principle includes the fact that data subjects should be informed how their personal data will be used and if the data has been breached.

Where the processing of personal data is based on consent, this will need to be demonstrable. Consent is one of the lawful bases for processing data, set out in Article 6. We will come back to this in the next section.

---

[6] See https://gdpr-info.eu/art-9-gdpr/

The principle also supports the rights of access, rectification, erasure, restriction of processing, portability and the right to object – collectively known as Data Subject Rights. These rights are a significant feature of the GDPR from the consumer perspective, but of less relevance to the data analyst.

Principle 2 - Purpose limitation
This principle prevents you from collecting data for one purpose and using it for another. For example, if you collected people's email addresses for a prize draw, you would not be allowed to add them to your mailing list unless that had been made clear to them (note that there are other restrictions on this as well).

Principle 3 – Data minimisation
Data minimisation means that you can't ask for lots and lots of data in the hope that some may be interesting. For example, a retailer may have valid reason to record if a customer is under or over the age of 21, but not the exact date of birth.

Adherence to this principle has caused changes to documents such as application forms and online registration.

Principle 4 – Accuracy
Accurate data is no longer a 'nice to have', but has become a legal requirement for personal data. Associated with this is the obligation that inaccurate personal data is rectified without 'undue delay'.[7]

Principle 5 – Storage limitation
Storage limitation is otherwise known as retention periods. These must be appropriate; for example, your dentist may keep records of your X-rays back for a few years, but do they really need to keep them back to childhood? On the other hand, insurers may legitimately keep some policy records for 50 years or more, to cover cases of illnesses resulting from exposure to toxic materials going back decades.

---

[7] See https://gdpr-info.eu/art-16-gdpr/

Some organisations are applying retention periods to different uses and roles. For example, the marketing team may only see personal data within a retention period of 18 months, whereas the legal team can see personal data stretching back seven years or more. This can be enforced by applying user profiles when logging into systems.

Principle 6 – Integrity and confidentiality
We have all seen media reports of confidential information being lost – not just by falling into the hands of hackers, but also in occurrences such as losing a laptop or USB stick. This has always been a risk for organisations, but it now carries a regulatory impact as well.

This principle is also behind the requirement to report a personal data breach if it's likely to result in a risk to people's rights and freedoms. Reporting must be done 'without undue delay and, where feasible, not later than 72 hours after having become aware of it'.[8]

Lawful bases for processing personal data
Article 6 of the GDPR also sets out the lawful bases for processing personal data:

a. Consent of the data subject

The ICO describe data subject consent for GDPR nicely:[9]

> Consent must be freely given; this means giving people genuine ongoing choice and control over how you use their data.
>
> Consent should be obvious and require a positive action to opt in. Consent requests must be prominent, unbundled

---

[8] See https://gdpr-info.eu/art-33-gdpr/

[9] Information Commissioner's Office, 'Consent' (as of April 2018), licenced under the Open Government Licence: https://ico.org.uk/for-organisations/guide-to-the-general-data-protection-regulation-gdpr/lawful-basis-for-processing/consent/

DATA ANALYST

from other terms and conditions, concise and easy to understand, and user-friendly.

Consent must specifically cover the controller's name, the purposes of the processing and the types of processing activity.

Explicit consent must be expressly confirmed in words, rather than by any other positive action.

There is no set time limit for consent. How long it lasts will depend on the context. You should review and refresh consent as appropriate.

This requirement for consent has caused problems for organisations with large mailing lists when the original sign up was:

- not recorded by the organisation, or can't be found; or
- was done on an opt-out, rather than an opt-in basis.[10]

> In June 2017, the pub chain, Wetherspoons, advised all customers on its database that it would cease sending them emails and would be deleting all the details that they held about them. The company advised also that it would instead use its website and social media to share news of promotions and special offers.
>
> At the time, it was widely reported that this was a pre-emptive step to avoid the effort required in meeting the GDPR requirements (which were then almost a year away from enforcement).

---

[10] Opt-out is when your agreement is assumed, unless you say that you don't agree. Opt-in is where you only receive material if you asked for it.

b. Necessary for the performance of a contract

The data processing is necessary:

- in relation to a contract which the data subject has entered into; or
- because the individual has asked for something to be done so they can enter into a contract.

This ties in with rights such as the 'right to be forgotten'. Individuals can request that an organisation deletes the information that they hold about them, but the organisation may have reason to decline this. For example, a mobile phone company where the customer is still in contract.

c. Necessary for compliance with a legal obligation

If data processing must occur in order to comply with a legal obligation, it is considered lawful. For example, when employers deduct income tax and National Insurance payments from employees (a legal obligation), they will also need to provide personal details of who they relate to.

Legal obligations can come from the law of any EU country.

d. To protect vital interests of a data subject or another person

Data processing to protect the vital interests of a data subject or another person only applies in cases of life and death, such as when an individual's medical history is disclosed to a hospital's A&E department treating them after a serious road accident.

e. Necessary for the performance of a task carried out in the public interest or in the exercise of official authority vested in the controller

Examples of data processing necessary for the performance of a task carried out in the public interest or in the exercise of official authority by the controller include crime reporting, preventive or occupational medicine and social care.

f. Legitimate interests

The category of legitimate interests covers cases where you need to be able to 'do your job', but the rationale isn't based on a specific purpose and doesn't fit into any of the other categories.

Helpfully, the ICO have taken the text of the regulation and broken it down into a three-part test,[11] to be applied in order:

- Purpose test – is there a legitimate interest behind the processing?
- Necessity test – is the processing necessary for that purpose?
- Balancing test – is the legitimate interest overridden by the individual's interests, rights or freedoms?

The 'purpose test' may seem to be redundant, as the test of 'legitimate interests' begins by asking if there is 'legitimate interest'! However, what it does is make you work out exactly why you want to do the activity, which then makes it easier to carry out the other two tests.

There are further conditions for special categories of data, detailed in Article 9, which are outside the scope of this book.

DATA SECURITY

Data analysts are entrusted with data – some of which will be personal data, but all of which must be looked after. This

---

[11] Article 6(1)(f) of the GDPR; Information Commissioner's Office, 'What is the "legitimate interests" basis?' (as of October 2018), licenced under the Open Government Licence: https://ico.org.uk/for-organisations/guide-to-the-general-data-protection-regulation-gdpr/legitimate-interests/what-is-the-legitimate-interests-basis/

section looks at two ways data analysts mitigate the risk of losing data. The first way looks at changing data so that they are not holding so much (or any) personal data. The other is more general guidance about reducing the chance of that data being taken.

Rendering a data subject no longer identifiable

The concept of personally identifying information lies at the core of the GDPR, but does not apply to data that 'does not relate to an identified or identifiable natural person or to data rendered anonymous in such a way that the data subject is no longer identifiable'.[12] Where a data subject can no longer be identified, then controllers do not need to provide those data subjects with access, rectification, erasure or data portability.

> On a related note, GDPR does not apply to personal data of the deceased, although some countries, notably Denmark, use local law to include this.[13]

There are three main ways of achieving this:

- data anonymisation (also known as data masking or data obfuscation);
- data encryption;
- data pseudonymisation.

Data anonymisation
There are several techniques for data anonymisation. The challenge is in retaining the informational value of the data for analysis. Techniques include:

---

[12] Recital 26 of GDPR: www.privacy-regulation.eu/en/recital-26-GDPR.htm

[13] See www.twobirds.com/en/in-focus/general-data-protection-regulation/gdpr-tracker/deceased-persons

Substitution Replacing data with random but authentic text. For example, we have a list of first names by gender, and replace the first names of policy holders with a name taken from the list. This is helpful to analysts who retain an understanding of the type of data in a field. One possible issue is that, in the event of a breach, it could create an impression that personal data has been lost.

Aggregation This reduces the level of detail in data to a level where the data is no longer able to uniquely identify a person, but can still provide valuable analysis. For example, when analysing customers in a shop, the exact date of birth could be generalised to age bands (for example, age 18–24, 25–29, 30–35, etc.). When considering addresses, the first part of the postcode alone (for example, SW1) could be used to identify where your customers live, without the need for a full address.

> **EXAMPLE OF DATA ANONYMISATION**
>
> Premium Bonds are issued by the NS&I, a government body. The monthly lists of high value prize winners include information about where they live.
>
> To protect winners' anonymity and help to keep their personal details confidential, they only list an area when there are at least 100,000 Premium Bond holders living there.
>
> If this is not the case, the following hierarchy is used until there is a level with at least 100,000 Premium Bond holders:
>
> - Level 1: Royal Mail postcode address file (PAF) town;
> - Level 2: county or local authority;
> - Level 3: government standard region;
> - Level 4: country.
>
> (Information from: www.nsandi.com/prize-checker)

Shuffling Data could be randomly shuffled within a column (for example, the dates of birth across all policy holders are swapped). However, if used in isolation, anyone with any knowledge of the original data can then apply a 'What if' scenario to the data set and then piece back together a real identity. The shuffling method is also open to being reversed if the shuffling algorithm can be deciphered. The fact that data in this case is no longer accurate is not a problem because the data is no longer considered to be personal data.

Number and date variance This is appropriate for financial and date related fields. For example, applying a variance of around +/- 10 per cent may still provide meaningful salary data. Dates of birth could be shifted by a number of days, masking the true dates but keeping the same (although shifted) distribution patterns. As with shuffling, we need not worry that this makes the data inaccurate.

Nulling out or deletion This approach is simple, but destroys the informational value of data and also makes it very obvious that the data has been masked. Dynamic data masking is where only some of the details are hidden, so that a customer service person sees the last four digits of a credit card number; but the system itself retains all the digits so that the transaction can be made.

Data encryption

This is often seen by business users as the 'easiest approach' to managing personal data, as security is added without losing any data, but encryption is a complex approach technically. Usually, a 'key' is required to view the data, but this raises the challenge of the key being obtained by unauthorised users, and those with access making unencrypted copies of the data.

Encryption usually affects the performance of the database or system that it is applied to, so organisations will generally identify specific data items to encrypt, rather than everything. Under GDPR, if there is a breach, but the data was encrypted, then there is no regulatory requirement to inform the data subjects. This is seen as a strong incentive for encryption, but there could remain a reputational impact if an unreported breach became public knowledge.

Data pseudonymisation

Pseudonymisation is a technique where directly identifying data is held separately and securely from processed data to ensure non-attribution. It can significantly reduce the risks associated with data processing while also maintaining the data's utility. As with encryption, pseudonymised data that is breached would not require a notification to the data subjects, but the same reputational risk noted above applies.

There are two ways in which pseudonymised data could be re-identified:

- The identifying data and the processed data are both obtained through a data breach.
- The processed data could be combined with other available information to identify the individuals.

The key distinction between pseudonymous data, which is regulated by the GDPR, and anonymous data, which is not, is whether the data can be re-identified with reasonable effort. GDPR considers pseudonymised data to be personal data if it could be attributed to a natural person by the reasonable use of additional information.

EXAMPLE OF RE-IDENTIFICATION

Consider flags such as gender, job title and salary band. By themselves, none of these could identify an individual in the UK:

- Knowing if a person is male or female gives around 30 million possibilities.
- Defining a job title as 'Member of Parliament' gives more than 600 possibilities.

> - The number of people with annual salaries above £140,000 per year is more than 100,000.
>
> However, if we consider female Members of Parliament earning more than £140,000 per year, we have only one possibility: the Prime Minister at the time of writing, Theresa May.
>
> GDPR would consider this grouping as personal data because the identification does not require a great amount of effort. Ministerial salaries are not confidential and can be accessed freely on the internet. The name of the Prime Minister is also publicly available information!

The UK implementation of GDPR adds an additional offence of intentionally or recklessly re-identifying individuals from anonymised or pseudonymised data. Offenders who knowingly handle or process such data are also guilty of an offence and the maximum penalty is an unlimited fine.

Data breaches

Once data analysts have been entrusted with other people's data, there is an obligation to take care of it. A scan of the news media will reveal many high-profile data breaches from large and respected companies; indeed, you may yourself have received an email or letter advising you that your account details might have been breached. Even the most competent organisations, in this respect, talk about *when* a breach happens rather than *if*.

> Breaches can occur accidentally through social means, as well as by malicious attack. Consider the following scenarios – maybe you have seen these yourself?

- A person making a purchase over the phone in a public place, giving out their credit card numbers (front and back) and the other associated data to make a valid transaction.

- The conscientious worker using their train journey home to get some work done, and not realising that the person next to them can read the document they are working on.

- Your email software's autocomplete function causing you to send a work email to a personal contact with the same first name.

Consider steps you could take to minimise the chance of being caught out in these ways:

- If you must give your details out over the phone, do it somewhere private.

- Screen filters are available for laptops and tablets, so you can only see the screen if you are looking straight at it.

- The traditional approach is to check and check again before you hit send for an email. Some companies have configured their email tools to generate a warning if the email is going to an address outside the corporate domain.

The frequency of data breaches means that public tolerance is beginning to increase in this regard, particularly where the organisation had good defences in place, reporting of the breach is prompt and support is given to those who are affected. For example, it is common for the breached company to provide an identity monitoring service, which will flag any indication that an individual is a victim of identity theft.

On the other hand, organisations that do not handle the situation well can find that their reputations are shattered in a very short time. Organisations adversely affected by a data breach may well decide that some of their data analysis falls outside their risk appetite (that is, the risk of something negative happening is considered to be higher than the benefit they get from the analysis) and they decide to hold less data and/or reduce their use of it.

> Find out what you should do if you were to lose your organisation's laptop or mobile phone. Is there a phone number that you should call or an address that should be emailed? If you had lost one or both devices, would you still be able to find those details?
>
> What if you lost your own phone? Could the person with your phone get access to your Facebook, Twitter, Instagram or LinkedIn apps? Could they get access to your online banking? Could they even spend your money if you've set up phone-based payments? Most modern phones allow remote wiping of data, but you would need to know how to do this and sometimes the method needs to be set up in advance.

DATA GOVERNANCE

> A Data Analyst function is to leverage data to take a nebulous question and refine it down to an exact one.
> (James Londal, Chief Data Officer, Hearts & Science)

For both the data analyst and their organisation, the best of use of time is to analyse data. However, as discussed in the previous chapters, data often requires extensive preparation before use.

The concept of data governance is to put in place people, processes and tools to ensure that there are people who are responsible, accountable, consulted and informed about data issues. Well-governed data is helpful to the data analyst if:

- It is documented, the source(s) of the data is identified and the data item is defined.
- The quality of the data item is known over a period of time.
- The journey of the data item from source to target is known.
- The people involved in the data (such as owners, stewards, subject matter experts) are identified.

Data governance is typically driven by a policy document, which will set out the organisation's approach to data. The activity to achieve the position described in the policy is then set out in more detailed policy documents, or through specific standards or controls.

A data management team

Historically, responsibility for data sat within the IT function because data issues would be considered as part of the systems and technologies where the data was found. Over time, organisations have set up dedicated data management functions, which often incorporate legacy management information (MI) and business intelligence (BI) teams alongside those responsible for building out data governance activities. More mature setups will have a central 'data office' under a Chief Data Officer (CDO).

Whatever the name, central data functions are often very small relative to the size of the organisation – having just one or two people is common. An exception is where data quality checking or a similar activity is centralised under the data function; but, even in these cases, there will be a small number of people focusing on data governance. Successful data offices can function with a small headcount because they work with many other people around the organisation.

Before we talk about using other people, let's find out more about the problems that a data management team looks to solve.

DATA QUALITY

In general language, we associate 'quality' with ideas such as being 'good', 'right' or 'correct'. Data analysts need to be more careful how they define things, so let's consider what 'data quality' means.

What does 'good' data quality mean and when is good, good enough?

'Good data quality' is a phrase often used, and most business stakeholders will make statements around 'the importance of good quality data', 'Six Sigma quality'[14] or 'everything must be 100 per cent accurate'. Conversely, 'bad data' is an easy thing to blame when business decisions have led to poor outcomes. Moreover, many people who spend their time working with data will have a natural desire to want to have all the data 'right'. This can cause such people to invest a great deal of time in fixing relatively minor issues.

> The time and resources that are spent fixing 'small' data issues are the time and resources that are *not* spent on fixing major issues and managing root causes.

This approach starts well, but ultimately fails due to the amount of effort required as more and more data issues are identified. A more structured approach to data quality considers these three steps:

1. define;
2. measure;
3. monitor.

---

[14] Six Sigma is a widely used process improvement methodology. The term comes from statistics, and represents near-perfection. In a Six Sigma process, there are just 3.4 defective features per million opportunities!

Defining data quality

We can describe how good data needs to be by using data quality dimensions.

> **WHAT ARE QUALITY DIMENSIONS?**
>
> In the context of data quality, dimensions refer to the attribute of the data that we are considering.

Typical data quality dimensions include:

- accuracy;
- appropriateness;
- timeliness (sometimes incorporated within appropriateness);
- completeness;
- uniqueness;
- validity;
- consistency.

Let's work through what they mean.

Accuracy This is what most people mean when talking about data quality. Accuracy can be thought of as 'correctness'.

Getting a single character error in an email address will likely cause the email not to go to the right place.[15] For example, it would be bizarre to consider that 15 out of 16 characters are correct, so it is 94 per cent accurate. Rather, we would say that the email address in this case is inaccurate.

---

15 An exception being gmail, which ignores full stops before the @; so b.cs@gmail.com would get to the same mailbox as bc.s@gmail.com.

Appropriateness This considers if data analysts are looking at data relevant to the problem they are trying to solve.

If a shop owner wants to measure customers that enter the shop, they could monitor the colour of customers' socks. This information could be 100 per cent accurate, but also entirely useless. Such data would be considered inappropriate.

When looking at large data sets, it is likely that much of the data will be useless for the task in hand. Being able to identify and extract useful data is one of the most challenging, and rewarding, parts of being a data analyst.

Timeliness Imagine that an ice cream seller is trying to estimate how much ice cream to purchase before a sunny day at the beach. It would be sensible to look at how much ice cream they had bought on previous occasions, and how much remained unsold. But if that ice cream seller looked at sales figures from six months earlier – an entirely different season – then the analysis would be misleading. This would be the case even if the data was highly accurate. This is an example of the timeliness dimension. Are we considering data in a relevant and useful timeframe?

At the extreme end of the timeliness spectrum, financial institutions involved in algorithmic and high-speed trading will require some data points to be within fractions of a second of the current time.

Completeness Completeness considers whether we have all the data that we need. This does not mean taking all the data available; as discussed for appropriateness, it is a key skill to pick out the useful data.

Some of the incorrect predictions made in recent general elections have been blamed on incomplete data, such as not considering voter patterns in remote areas of the country. In a corporate context, common causes of incomplete data are when data has been copied from a spreadsheet (missing some rows or columns) and pasted elsewhere; or when a data transfer between systems has stopped before completion, so that not all of the data is found in the recipient system.

> On the night of 18 September 2008, a first-year law associate supporting the Barclays acquisition of assets from the stricken Lehman Brothers company, reformatted a Microsoft Excel spreadsheet of critical contracts to be assumed and assigned in bankruptcy on the closing date of the Lehman/Barclays sale. This work was done long after normal business hours, just after 11.30 p.m.
>
> On 19 September, the law firm produced the list of contracts based on the associate's work the night before. There was a problem. The list contained 179 contracts that should not have been included. The sale closed on 22 September, with the overinclusive list of contracts.
>
> The mistake was caught on 1 October. According to the various affidavits posted at court, the associate did not notice that the 179 contracts were marked as 'hidden' in Excel, and did not realise that those entries became 'un-hidden' when he globally reformatted the document.
>
> The law firm had to file a motion before the bankruptcy court asking for relief from the final sale order due to mistake or excusable neglect.
> (This account is based on Mystal 2008)

Uniqueness This refers to having records corresponding to 'real world' items. This itself can be subjective.

> The Office for National Statistics (ONS) data for the most popular boys' baby names in 2016 listed Muhammad as the eighth most popular name. However, this methodology does not include other spellings of what is effectively the same name, so Mohammed appeared in 31st place, Mohammad was 68th and other variants were also counted separately.

> Combining these versions would take the name into first place. The ONS provide their own response to the question: https://visual.ons.gov.uk/the-popularity-of-the-name-muhammadmohammedmohammad/

Validity Validity considers whether the data meets some predefined criteria, but does not consider if the data is 'correct' or 'accurate'. It is possible for data to be both valid and inaccurate.

The benefit of considering validity is that it is much easier to test for validity than for correctness. Validity can be expressed by some simple rules or constraints, whereas accuracy requires us to have the 'correct answer' to be checked against. This means that validity is also useful as a pre-check of data.

Recall when you last made an online purchase using a credit card. If you made an error in entering the credit card number, so there were too few or too many digits, the website would normally give you an error message – without checking the actual credit card number. The validity test of number of digits is enough for this first pass.

Consistency This uses logic across multiple sources of the same or equivalent data to identify possible errors.

A retailer may compare a customer's billing and delivery addresses. These do not have to be the same, but, where they are not, there could be an extra control put in place to ensure that the delivery address is legitimate. Taking this a step further, if we store people's dates of birth in one place; and their ages in another, then – assuming we have the correct current date – we should be able to test that the dates of birth and ages are consistent.

Another instance of consistency is where data is moved or copied from one place to another. For example, a system outputs data to a spreadsheet, which is merged with another spreadsheet. Each of these 'jumps' is known as a transformation, and each transformation carries a risk of introducing errors to the data. Consistency is when errors are not introduced.

Putting it all together The relevant data quality dimensions (or a combination of them) will change depending on the nature of the data and what the analyst wants to achieve with it.

It is vital that data analysts engage with stakeholders to understand what they require from their data. This may not be immediately apparent, and can often require some extended conversation or questioning to tease out what is truly of interest.

Measuring data quality

Once data analysts know what they are looking for, they can think about measuring it. Each dimension requires a different approach for measurement – and some of them can be difficult to measure.

Table 4.1 suggests approaches for each of the dimensions just discussed, but this is not an exhaustive list and there may be specific factors that apply to particular use cases.

Monitoring data quality

Having defined and measured our data quality, we now move to the third step: monitoring the outputs of the data quality measurement activity.

While sharing the raw data quality measurements may expose the correct and relevant numbers, the real purpose of doing so is to assess where action needs to be taken and to drive activity that mitigates or resolves the issue, or, if no action is to be taken, acknowledges that the lack of action is a conscious decision (for example, choosing to allocate resources to other activities).

Table 4.1 Suggested approaches for data quality dimensions

Dimension	Suggested approach
Accuracy	Measuring accuracy requires that the user of the data has a way of determining what the 'correct' value is for the data. The most common measurement of data accuracy would be in terms of percentage of error (for example, 100 fields were rekeyed into a system and checked back to source. Two incorrect fields implies a 98 per cent accuracy score). Alternatively, it can be defined by a measure such as currency, temperature or weight (for example, the amount of money in the shop's till must be within 99.5 per cent of the amount per the receipts).
Appropriateness and timeliness	The data user must have defined their data requirements (timeliness being specifically about the appropriate timeframe) and the measure is a simple yes/no, or proportions of records which are yes/no, in terms of meeting those requirements.
Completeness	Once the data analyst has defined how big the data set should be (i.e. what constitutes 100 per cent), the completeness score is the percentage of the data set that the analyst has.

(Continued)

Table 4.1 (Continued)

Dimension	Suggested approach
Uniqueness	Having normalised the data, the analyst needs to identify the proportion of data items post-normalisation to the initial size of the set. For example, if you have a list of 100 names, where three of the entries are 'Mr J Smith', 'MrJ Smith' and 'J Smith Esq.', and all the other names are unique, this would imply a uniqueness score of 98 per cent.[16]
Validity	Validity requires rules to be set in advance, such as all credit card numbers must have 16 digits; or all postcodes start and end with a letter. The validity score is the percentage of records that meet the rules. Unlike accuracy, a single rule breach makes a record invalid, so the score would not be affected if a single record breached more than one validity rule.
Consistency	Consistency assumes that you have two or more presentations of the same data. 100 per cent consistent data would be the same values across each of them.

Data quality scores or measurements provide useful insight when measured over a period of time. For example:

---

[16] If you are wondering why is this 98 per cent and not 97 per cent, then consider that the three names consolidate to one, so only two terms are duplicates or non-unique.

- A small but steady deterioration in quality may not be noticed from month to month, but the trend can be observed (and so acted upon) over several months.
- A large change in the quality score may indicate a new issue (perhaps an underlying system has stopped working).

Showing your outputs through a dashboard is a powerful method of generating buy-in from the data users and management. Dashboard design is outside the scope of this book, but a fundamental principle is that it must be designed to be meaningful to the audience, even if this is at the expense of sharing all the information you would like to share.

Improving data quality

The steps taken so far expose data issues; some are more important than others, and some are more complex or expensive to fix than others. The people who help data analysts to deal with these issues are discussed in the next section, but analysts need to give those people something to work with.

Issue trackers An issue tracker is used to record data issues and their implications, together with progress towards remediation. As usual, there are commercial tools available such as the workflow tools as commonly used by IT support desks and also more focused data governance tools, but a basic tracker can be operated successfully in Microsoft Excel.

An issue tracker should include:

- A unique identifier for the issue.
- A description of the issue (data analysts may wish to additionally have a shorter 'headline').
- The impacts of the issue: people, process, cost (these may change over time as more is discovered about the issue and its resolution). Being able to put a financial impact on an issue is an extremely powerful way of driving a resolution – and of demonstrating the value of the analyst who resolved it.

- Who and when: the issue was raised by; the issue last updated by; issue closed by; and key stakeholders.
- Target date(s) for remediation of the issue (for example, it may be necessary to fix a report by a specific due date).
- The status of the issue (open, resolved, mitigated, dropped).
- A risk rating for the issue (red, amber, green).

It is good practice not to delete items from the tracker. Sometimes issues may be closed on the grounds of being immaterial, but then, when another event arises at a later time, these can be linked when considering what action to take.

Linking this improving of data quality to monitoring it, data analysts can create a dashboard of issues trackers: this could demonstrate their success at closing data issues, and the financial benefits (money saved, or money made) from doing so.

ENGAGING WITH THE ORGANISATION – THE DATA COMMUNITY

Many data quality issues can be categorised as 'problem exists between chair and keyboard' (PEBCAK), but while people may often be the cause of issues, they will also lead you to solutions.

Even where there is no formal data governance in place in an organisation, there are often pockets of conscientious good practice. This may take the form of a post-data entry review or reconciliation, sometimes known as 'four eyes testing'. The flaw here is that the remediation effort is unlikely to have considered the risk, impact and cost of resolution – so resources may not be used in an optimal way.

To engage people, they have to be given defined roles – roles that are viable alongside their existing day jobs. Putting too much work onto individuals will simply lead to work not being done, and data governance work, which may not yet have established its value, will be the first not to get done.

We will now define these roles together with some ways to help individuals fulfil them, and some causes why this might not be happening. The roles may have different names in different organisations, but it should still be possible for the data analyst to identity them through their activities.

> This is a story about four people named Everybody, Somebody, Anybody and Nobody.
>
> There was an important job to be done and Everybody was sure that Somebody would do it.
>
> Anybody could have done it, but Nobody did it.
>
> Somebody got angry about that, because it was Everybody's job.
>
> Everybody thought Anybody could do it, but Nobody realized that Everybody wouldn't do it.
>
> It ended up that Everybody blamed Somebody when Nobody did what Anybody could have.
>
> (Attributed to Charles Osgood's poem, *A Poem About Responsibility*)

Data user

The first business role is that of a data user: anyone making use of data in a business. Data analysts can't give specific responsibilities to data users in the organisation because they usually won't have the resources to do so. They can, however, create an environment where data users are *able* to highlight data issues, and analysts are likely to find that data users around the business will have a backlog of issues to share.

What can help a data user to succeed?
A clear and non-complex way for data users to share knowledge of issues and be informed about progress of their issue and, where appropriate, mitigation or resolution.

What can prevent a data user from helping?
A complex or little known process to flag data issues. A lack of response and, even where a mitigation or resolution has been found, poor communication of this.

Data steward

The next role is commonly referred to as a data steward. These are some of the most important allies that data analysts will have in the data community. These people understand the systems and processes that support data inside out, back to front and in reverse.

The data stewards will be the ones who can advise whether a problem is truly complex, and may also know the underlying issues. Where data flows between multiple sources, bringing together the relevant data stewards will greatly help the process of root cause analysis.

> **WHAT IS ROOT CAUSE ANALYSIS?**
>
> Root cause analysis is a problem-solving approach that traces a problem all the way back to its source.
>
> The major benefit of this approach is that the root cause may have triggered other issues – as yet unidentified – and so fixing the problem at its root will resolve those issues as well, improving quality more widely.

Indicators that a person is likely to be a strong data steward
People known in the business for their technical or subject matter expertise to whom others will go for support. They will often have their own list of data quality issues that they would like to address.

What can go wrong when working with a data steward?
The data function not engaging with data stewards; or inability to get some quick wins (these are needed to gain the stewards' confidence).

Data owner

The third role is that of the data owner. The data owner must be someone of sufficient seniority to make decisions and authorise budget or resource as required. Data owners may delegate much of their activity to their stewards, but they cannot pass on the responsibility or accountability.

Data owners are sometimes referred to as business owners, or even business data owners, to differentiate them from the IT professionals who have some level of system ownership.

Indicators of a successful data owner
A senior individual who is engaged and can advocate for good data practice with their peer group; someone who knows the business politics well and can help to navigate it.

Indicators of an ineffective data owner
A role holder who is there in name only; no budget or influence to be able to drive or sign off resolution activity; anyone who uses the phrases 'gold plating'[17] or 'boiling the ocean'[18] when it is proposed to enhance processes or control activities.

Governance committees

Engaging with multiple data owners and data stewards will quickly become very time-consuming, and prioritising the resolution of data issues will also be challenging unless you can bring the stakeholders together.

---

[17] Translation: things work well enough as they are, and you are trying to spend resources making them better than they need to be.

[18] Translation: this sounds like a lot of work, so I'm going to say it's impossible.

The senior governance committee for data should consist of the most significant data owners. An associated working group would comprise the most significant data stewards. In both cases, other attendees can attend by invitation. However, the working group should not be put in place until the senior governance committee agrees that it is needed. If not, then there is a risk that the working group has little to do and it fizzles out.

Terms of reference will need to be set out for each group, which include:

- committee purpose;
- membership and quorum;
- meeting frequency;
- lines of escalation and delegation;
- budget responsibility (if there is any);
- standing agenda.

It is critical that these committees are able to manage real issues early on so that credibility is established. The majority of failures in this respect are when the committee members do not feel that the group is adding value.

Given that the ownership of data lies in the business, a successful committee will have input from its business members. A meeting must not consist only of the central data function describing what they have, or haven't, done.

DATA PROVENANCE

Where does data come from, and how does a data analyst know that it is any good, and that it hasn't been corrupted on the way in? In all but the most simple organisations, data will enter from many sources, and move through many other data sources before being consumed. For example, customer data could be entered by shop staff into one system, by the call centre team into another one and directly by the customers themselves when shopping online. Changes to data (for example, resolving complaints) could subsequently be made by another team entirely.

Data could then flow out of those data entry systems into a data warehouse. Some may have a direct feed; others may need to be exported into a database or spreadsheet before being imported to the warehouse; yet others may require manual rekey into another system before import. Once extracted from the warehouse into a spreadsheet, that spreadsheet could be manipulated in all sorts of ways before being used to make a business decision.

Data lineage mappings

A solution to this uncertainty is the creation of a data lineage map. These provide a visual representation of how data gets from source to its usage. Mapping all data flows in an organisation can be a mammoth task, and the map produced will be so complex as to be unusable. Instead, data analysts can create mappings that relate to particular business activities.

The simple lineage in Figure 4.1 shows what happens when a customer buys an item online. Having ordered through the website, their data will go into a customer order database; however, some of this data goes direct (for example, what they ordered and when), while their billing data could go via a credit card company,[19] and the address data also needs to go to the firm carrying out the delivery.

Finding and documenting the content

This can be the most interesting part of the process. Around your organisation, people know how to do their own jobs; engaging with these people enables you to understand the processes and join them up into a 'big picture'. Frequently, no

---

[19] The Payment Card Industry Data Security Standard (PCI DSS) is a very stringent standard for organisations working with credit card data.

Figure 4.1 A simple data lineage map

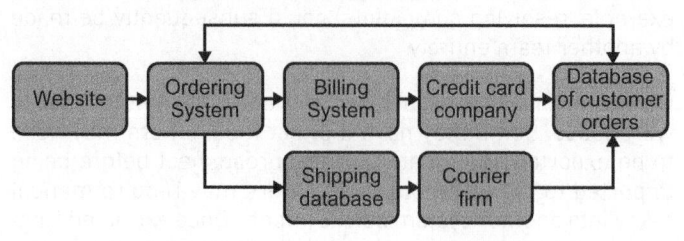

Website → Ordering System → Billing System → Credit card company → Database of customer orders

Ordering System → Shipping database → Courier firm → Database of customer orders

one in the business will have seen how complex the entire process is from end to end.

> This author was involved in a data lineage exercise relating to a particular business process. The initial response was that the lineage must have got something wrong as it was too big. Once satisfied that it was accurate, the team looked at each component of the process and found ways to simplify them. A positive result of this activity was the retirement of several spreadsheets; and doing so reduced the number of opportunities to introduce errors.

This role is best suited to a trained business analyst, who will have specific skills in terms of eliciting this information and documenting it properly. Some tips for data analysts doing this themselves include:

- Take the time to work with the business users – you want to extract all the detail.

- There is almost always a 'right way' of doing a process and the 'real way' that things get done, especially when there are exceptions. A good trigger question is to ask: 'Do you always do things this way?'

Tools such as Microsoft Visio are often used to build data lineages. These outputs are frozen at a period in time, so it is important to have a regular review cycle. More recently, commercial tools have been developed that support collaboration; for example, any business user can update the data lineage and, once approved, the revised lineage is available to all. Some tools are also able to be linked directly to systems and can hence generate part of the data flows for analysts.

SUMMARY

In this chapter, we have seen how interest in and use of data and analytics has increased over past years, and how this has both positive and negative effects on the business. Governments have introduced legal and regulatory responses, most recently the GDPR, which has been in force since 25 May 2018. GDPR does not stop organisations working with personal data, but does require that care is taken as to why, where and how it is used.

The processes covered in this chapter, along with other best practice considerations for data analysts, described how data analysts need to be able to define, measure and monitor data quality, and appreciate the importance of communicating and tracking issues so that required actions are taken.

5 CAREER PROGRESSION OPPORTUNITIES

There are several career paths that you can take on the road to becoming a data analyst. Sometimes it is an early career choice and you may have decided to specialise from day one. More often, data analyst is a role that you move into as part of your career development, perhaps because an opportunity presents itself, perhaps because you enjoy the challenge, perhaps because you become fascinated by what you can learn from data and how data can shape the way in which an organisation operates. This chapter looks at the ways you can become a data analyst, the opportunities and challenges of this career path and how you can continue to develop your career. It includes some real-world stories showcasing the range of backgrounds and career moves that can lead to you a career in data analysis.

The contributors to this book work in sectors including consultancy, industry, finance and higher education. We all regard ourselves as data analysts, but what we do varies, and we all took a different route to arrive at where we are. Your route to becoming a data analyst is likely to be just as interesting. If you decide that the data analyst role is for you, we hope you enjoy the journey and the role as much as we do.

> Just a reminder – we are talking in this book about someone who works with data, analyses data, finds meaning in data, draws conclusions from data and shares that information and knowledge with the data stakeholders. We are not talking about being a business

> analyst or a business modeller, which are different roles, although there is sometimes an overlap between the role of the data analyst and the role of the business analyst.

THE CHANGING ROLE OF THE DATA ANALYST

This is an exciting time in the data world, particularly for data analysts. With the arrival of Big Data, data analysts face a whole range of new challenges and opportunities. Events are moving faster than ever before, and this is not a career where you can operate on autopilot! If you decide to become a data analyst, you will need to be committed to continually extending and developing your skills to stay current in a rapidly changing field. For that reason, there's a lot of talk in this chapter about continuous professional development (CPD) and ways to develop and extend your skills.

> The traditional view of a data analyst is to collect and analyse data to support business decisions. But a good data analyst does more. A good data analyst has the ability to communicate what story the data is telling so that their clients and partners make the right decisions.
> (Duncan Watkins, Senior Consultant, Forrester)

CAREER OPPORTUNITIES

Chapter 2 looked at the kind of tasks data analysts carry out and the key industries where data analysts work. Here, we look at the roles and career paths open to data analysts.

Career paths for data analysts

As Chapter 2 explained, there are a wide range of possible careers for someone with data analyst skills. In this section we look in a bit more detail at some of the most common career paths for data analysts. Some roles, such as those in data analytics and data mining, tend to have a greater focus on mathematical and statistical analysis skills, while other roles might focus more on the business environment, visualisation and operational reporting.

Working with business intelligence

Business intelligence means providing managers at all levels in the company, but particularly at middle and senior management levels, with the information they need to manage and grow the organisation. Data analysts working in a business intelligence environment for a large company might be involved in working with data from data warehouses, analysing trends and presenting information. A data analyst working for a smaller company might cover several roles; for example, they may be involved in identifying, together with management, the key performance indicators (KPIs) of a company, helping to develop a dashboard to present these KPIs to managers, analysing and visualising the outcomes from the data, making predictions based on the data and presenting their findings to management. They might also find themselves involved in training end users to understand and interpret the data they share with them.

HOW I BECAME A DATA ANALYST (A)

My career in data analysis has been more of a gradual journey than a conscious career choice. I moved to the UK in my early 20s and started working in junior data entry positions in the legal and financial services sectors. At first, I wanted to study for a career in IT network security, but the temptation of quick salary increases combined with challenging analytical problems and the gratification of influencing the strategy of a very large UK insurance company persuaded me to stay in data analysis. I had started part-time distance-learning university studies in computing and amended my module choices to include more statistical courses. Formal training and self study taught me to use a

> number of the common software tools, while work-based courses and on-the-job training gave me an understanding of communication styles and project management. Nearly 20 years later, I now work as an independent analytics consultant in financial risk management – but I'm still on my journey towards being better at data analysis.

Working with data analytics and data mining
This role overlaps with the business intelligence role, but if you are working as a data analyst with a focus on data mining, you are likely to be working with large data sets and using data mining algorithms to find patterns in data. Data mining is linked to data warehouses, and you might find that you take on more than one role and become involved in the management or development of the data warehouse. Data analysts working in this role, or working with complex data, are sometimes referred to as data scientists. Data analysts working as data scientists are likely to be working for large companies or government organisations or may be involved in scientific or medical research.

Working with Big Data
Big Data analytics is one of the fastest growing and most rapidly changing areas of data analysis and is likely to be a key sector in the future. Data analysts working with Big Data need to be able to deal with high volumes of data in a variety of formats, and also need to be able to work with sophisticated analysis tools. Big Data analytics applies to social media data and uses techniques such as sentiment analysis and text mining, but also covers sensor data and other forms of Big Data. It often involves real-time analysis and reporting, and some people might argue that the role of a Big Data analyst is very different from data analysts working with traditional data analysis. Tools and techniques change rapidly in this field, and data analysts will find that they are constantly extending and developing their skill sets.

Working with data assurance and data quality

Data analysis requires an understanding of the quality of the data that is being used. As a data analyst working in the field of data quality, you might use sampling techniques to examine the data, to verify what data is being collected and where and how the data is collected. You might have a role in evaluating the data and deciding how it can be used as input to support further analysis. This might be a specialist role, but often these tasks will form part of the work of the data analyst. Data analysts tend to feel an obligation to verify the quality of the data they are working with – on the rubbish in, rubbish out principle.

Mixed analytics

The changing role of the data analyst means that you may work in a variety of roles, perhaps all at the same time or at different stages of your career. Some data analysts specialise, for example, in data mining analytics, but many data analysts deal with different sorts of data and different types of analysis. Some people work in a role that combines data analyst skills with other skills and responsibilities, and some data analysts have a number of roles during their careers; have a look at the 'How I became a data analyst' boxes in this chapter. Some people move into roles that are not directly related to data analysis, but where their experience of data analysis provides them with a useful skill set. You may decide to specialise, but things are changing so rapidly that it is a good idea to have a range of skills and abilities in order to allow you to adapt to wherever the data industry goes next. Whichever career path you take, you will need to continually update and extend your skills.

What kind of jobs are there for someone with data analyst skills?

Data analyst skills open up a range of job opportunities and it is important to recognise that roles overlap. Even if you are primarily a data scientist, you might find that part of your role includes elements of the data architect role. You might find that a role one company calls operational research is called data analysis in another company, or that a role you would describe as a data scientist has a different job title. These are just some examples, and you will find that roles and the way roles are defined varies between companies. The important thing is to check the job specification and see what the role involves.

To give you an idea of the kind of careers that might be available, these are some examples of jobs directly related to the data analyst role:

- **Data analyst/data scientist/Big Data analyst:** the kind of thing just discussed, working in fields such as business intelligence, data analysis, data mining, Big Data analytics. For example, a data analyst working for a large retail company might analyse purchasing patterns looking at the associations between customer purchases and customer characteristics and identifying which items are usually purchased in combination with other items. Next time you look for an item at a supermarket and find it on the bottom shelf of the display, a data analyst is probably responsible for ensuring that this particular item is displayed in this particular location.

- **Operational research:** this can cover a range of activities, but usually relates to supporting decision-making through analysis. In some companies, this role may be seen as different from the data analyst role, but in other companies, it may be regarded as very similar.

- **Analytical officer/chief analytical officer:** this role is pretty much what the name suggests, someone who is responsible for the data analysis needed by a company. Sometimes this role includes other analytical responsibilities and may be wider than data analysis. The chief analytical officer is usually a senior role in a company.

These are some examples of jobs that might include a data analyst role – where you might be expected to have good data analysis skills, but data analysis is not the main focus of the job:

- **Data consultant:** acting as a data consultant requires the ability to handle a range of different tasks, which may include systems analysis, data management and data analytics. Data analysis skills are likely to be an important part of this role, but not its main focus.

- **Data architect:** someone who is responsible for analysing the data that a company holds and how the company works with that data. The data architect is responsible for developing strategies for managing data, integrating data where necessary and ensuring that data is available to the end users and other stakeholders. The data architect role focuses more on the nature and distribution of data as opposed to the more statistical and mathematical focus of a data scientist. A data architect will usually have a track record of working with and understanding data, and data architect is often a more senior role.

- **Data engineer:** this is similar to the data architect role, but is usually more technical. The data engineer role focuses more on working with data and databases, and implementing data policies, rather than on making strategic decisions about data.

- **Business analyst:** the business analyst role is not the same as the data analyst role, but a successful business analyst requires data analysis skills and people sometimes move between this role and the data analyst role.

These are some examples of jobs which at first sight might not seem to be linked to the data analyst role, but often require a data analysis skill set:

- **Business innovator/business transformation manager:** this might not seem to be a data analyst role, but look at the 'How I became a data analyst' boxes in this chapter for more insight. Data analysis skills are an important part of many roles.

- **Project manager:** managing a large project requires good analysis skills, but does not usually require the specialist analytical skills of, for example, a data scientist.
- **Logistics manager:** a logistics manager is usually involved in managing the flow of goods and services, handling complex data and analysing and resolving problems. Understanding and analysing data are an important part of the logistics manager's skill set, but are only part of the role.

BUILDING A CAREER AS A DATA ANALYST: GETTING STARTED

In Chapter 2, you read about the role, key tasks and skills that a data analyst requires. In this section we look at the sort of qualifications that can help you to build a career as a data analyst. Later on in this chapter, we will look at CPD and how you can combine formal academic qualifications with the soft skills that a data analyst needs to succeed.

The Skills Framework for the Information Age

If you are involved in information systems management at any level, you have probably heard of the SFIA. SFIA is an international skills framework that describes the professional skills and competencies that individuals and organisations need to have or need to develop to succeed in the information age. Qualifications such as the BCS Data Analyst Apprenticeship Scheme are designed with reference to SFIA. If you are thinking of doing a specialist data analyst qualification, it is worth checking the skills and accreditation offered against the professional skills and competencies described in SFIA.

Getting started

There are a number of ways to start your career as a data analyst. As you can see from the career stories in this chapter, a lot of data analysts do not set out to become data analysts and only specialise later in their careers. You may go, or have gone, straight into a data analyst role on leaving education, or you may find that your job means that you are working as an entry level data analyst and are learning data analyst skills on the job. The nature of the data analyst role means that if you want to progress in your chosen career, you would be expected to have some formal qualifications to demonstrate your skills and competence. One way to achieve this is to take additional qualifications part-time, but you could also decide to complete an on-the-job professional qualification, which might then allow you to continue on and achieve further qualifications. BCS, The Chartered Institute for IT offers training within in the workplace through the BCS Data Analyst Apprenticeship Scheme.

> ### HOW I BECAME A DATA ANALYST (B)
>
> When I started my IT career in IT infrastructure support, I had no understanding or appreciation of data analysis. Over time I became an IT instructor, and this provided me with my first opportunity to help people develop small IT database systems, thus expanding my own data skills. As my career progressed into systems development, IT consultancy and IT management, my skills and use of data grew, but purely within the realms of design and reporting rather than analysis. It wasn't until I started to work in business improvement that I began to develop my analytical data skills in order to help businesses get more value from their data. After completing my MBA dissertation, on the use of data modelling to predict customers at risk of falling into debt, I cemented my reputation as a data analyst. I now work as a business transformation manager and use a variety of business improvement, IT and data analysis skills to help my organisation improve, and, while data analysis is an important part of my role, it is very much used alongside other skills and disciplines to support my work.

What is the Data Analyst Apprenticeship Scheme?

The Data Analyst Apprenticeship Scheme is an apprenticeship qualification. It is recognised as a Level 4 qualification equivalent to a Level 4 National Vocational Qualification (NVQ) or to a Higher National Certificate (HNC). The Data Analyst Apprenticeship Scheme is designed for people who want to get a qualification while they are working.

How does the Data Analyst Apprenticeship Scheme work?

The Data Analyst Apprenticeship Scheme is run by BCS in conjunction with employers. What this means is that you study for the apprenticeship mainly in the workplace and you would need to have the support of your employer to join the scheme. The qualification is intended to take 24 months to complete. During that time, you will complete the Certificate in Data Analysis Tools and the Diploma in Data Analysis Concepts. You must complete both the Certificate and the Diploma to complete the apprenticeship, although it may be possible to gain an exemption from some elements. The full specification is available from the BCS website at www.bcs.org, but briefly, you will learn about data integration and data preparation, industry standard tools and the data life cycle, the different types of data and data architectures, data analysis tasks, data quality issues and compliance and ethical issues.

The apprenticeship is assessed in several ways. You will complete a number of tasks, including preparing a portfolio of evidence, completing a project, having an interview with an assessor and completing a final, timed multiple choice question (MCQ) test. You will also need a reference from your employer. Before you start the apprenticeship, you should discuss with your employer exactly what you will be required to do.

What are the entry requirements?

The entry requirements vary depending on the agreement with your employer, but the apprenticeship usually requires five GCSEs or equivalent and a relevant Level 3 qualification or successful completion of an aptitude test. An A Level is a Level 3 qualification and so is a Level 3 NVQ. For suitable applicants who do not have a Level 3 qualification, success in the aptitude test could be accepted in its place. Again, you will need to discuss the entry qualifications with your employer.

How will the Data Analyst Apprenticeship Scheme help my career?

Completing the Data Analyst Apprenticeship Scheme will give you a recognised Level 4 qualification that is mapped to the internationally recognised SFIA. The material you study will give you a solid foundation in data analysis and can provide you with the basis to continue on to get further qualifications.

Higher education qualifications for the data analyst role

A higher education qualification does not necessarily mean a BSc or BA degree. There are a range of international qualifications, and there are also UK qualifications such as the HNC and Higher National Diploma (HND). In this section, however, we are looking at honours degrees such as a BSc Hons or BA Hons or a Masters level degree. Some data analysts will go on to achieve further qualifications, such as a PhD.

Which is the best degree subject for a data analyst?

Do not chose a course because of its title. Look at what is taught on the degree and what modules you will study. There is a wide range of possible degree titles, but some degrees that are most likely to be relevant are:

- **Data science:** data science degrees are offered by a number of UK universities, but are not yet as widely available as more traditional qualifications such as the BSc in computer science. Data science degrees usually emphasise the mathematical and statistical elements and the use of analysis tools. As data science degrees are not yet very common, and as you may not make the decision to specialise until towards the end of your degree studies, you might choose to take a traditional computing degree and then go on to specialise at Masters level, perhaps doing an MSc in data science.

- **Mathematics and statistics:** this may be offered as a separate statistics course or as a combined mathematics and statistics course. If you study a mathematics degree and you know you want to be a data analyst, make sure you are also covering statistics. Some universities may offer degrees that combine computing with another subject, such as mathematics and computing or statistics and computing.

- **Business information systems or business computing or similar:** these degrees cover a range of topics and the content of the degree varies between universities, so make sure you read the degree specification. To become a data analyst, you want to be confident that you are covering topics which will give you the analytical skills you will need.

- **Computer science or computing science or another computing-related degree qualification:** these awards will give you a grounding in computing concepts, but some topics will be more relevant than others. If you already know that you want to be a data analyst, check the specification to make sure the course is covering the topics you want to study. Topics such as database design and development, data mining, data management, statistical analysis, operational research, mathematics, Big Data analytics, project management and data visualisation are all useful skills for a data analyst. Most degree courses also include modules that will help you to develop the soft skills you will need to succeed, such as communication and team working.

There are a number of other degree courses that might be relevant, such as economics, and some courses will include teaching on topics relevant to the data analyst, such as Big Data and Big Data analytics. Check what you will be studying on the degree course and talk to the admissions tutors to make sure you fully understand what your course will cover.

> **HOW I BECAME A DATA ANALYST (C)**
>
> When I started out, I hadn't heard much about analytics or the role of a data analyst. I had studied market research in my MBA and was quite keen to pursue primary research. I wasn't a believer in secondary research which most data analysts deal with. I got headhunted by a couple of PhD fellows who wanted to up-skill a few people as there was a lack of experienced data analysts in the city. From a small team, I soon moved into a 1100 employee analytics centre of excellence. I started my data analyst role in pricing. Later on, I moved to banking and used my data skills to solve problems that our customers face. Gradually, I moved into consulting and now have worked as an analyst, project manager and modeller. It's been 15 years and as I look back, I wonder how a person who did an advertising internship ended up as an analyst.

As mentioned earlier in this chapter, a lot of data analysts don't start out as data analysts. If you are considering a career as a data analyst, but have not completely made up your mind, or want to keep your options open, consider a degree such as computer science or mathematics and then take a specialist qualification afterwards.

I did a degree in a different subject; can I still be a data analyst?

Of course. Having a degree in a different subject does not stop you becoming a data analyst. One of the authors of this book has a first degree in English. A degree shows an ability to study at a certain level and you can acquire the specialist skills you will need through further study and professional development. If you read the career stories in this chapter, you will see that many professional data analysts never set out to be data analysts.

Should I study a Masters degree?

An MSc can be a useful way of acquiring specialist skills, particularly if your first degree was not relevant to your role as data analyst. Some data analysts have Masters level qualifications, usually in a relevant subject such as Big Data or data science or statistical analysis, and some data analysts go on to achieve PhDs, often while working on a data analysis project. Most Masters degrees can be studied part-time. On the other hand, a lot of data analysts prefer to get professional or technical qualifications rather than academic qualifications; you will need to decide what would be most helpful for you, and we suggest that you look at the later section of this chapter, 'Is this role for me?', to decide which skills and qualifications will most help you in your role.

Graduate training schemes

As the name suggests, a graduate training scheme is a scheme where graduates are recruited by companies to train for a particular role – in this case, that of data analyst. Terms and conditions differ between organisations, but, generally, you can expect to earn a graduate salary and to receive on-the-job training with the expectation that you are likely to be offered a permanent post once you have successfully completed the training and probation period. Some companies will also support you in gaining further job-related qualifications. Graduate training schemes are offered by a wide range of organisations, including government bodies. On the whole, it tends to be the larger companies who offer graduate training schemes and you can look on company websites for information. University careers centres will have information about the different types of companies and schemes that are on offer, and will point you in the direction of recruitment agencies that specialise in this area.

BUILDING A CAREER AS A DATA ANALYST: DEVELOPING YOUR ROLE

In this section we look at the ways in which you can develop in your career as a data analyst and acquire additional skills and qualifications.

What is continuous professional development?

CPD is a key part of building your career profile. It is the process of learning, reflecting on your learning and continuing to update your knowledge and skills. Chapter 2 talked about the need for data analysts to deal with new challenges and to be prepared to adapt to developments in the data world. In a changing field such as data analysis, qualifications and experience can quickly become out of date. The reason that professional development is described as 'continuous' is because it is expected to be a process that continues throughout your career.

- The first step in the CPD process is an audit of your skills and knowledge. People are often surprised to recognise how much they already know.
- Once you have established what you know and what skills and qualifications you have, you can move on to identifying any gaps in your knowledge and areas that you wish to develop further, perhaps related to what you currently do, perhaps related to what you hope to do in the future.
- The next stage is to plan your professional development activities, identifying what you need to do to achieve the goals you have set yourself.
- This is followed by completion of the professional development activities.
- Followed by the final step, where you review what you have learnt and reflect on what you have achieved.
- This leads to starting the process again: auditing your skills and knowledge to help you to identify other areas for development.

CPD is something you should expect to do throughout your professional career. One common theme in all the 'How I became a data analyst' stories in this chapter is that the learning process never stops.

CPD includes documenting what you have learnt, usually by creating a portfolio of CPD activities. There are two good reasons to document your professional development. The first is that this helps you to reflect on what you have learnt, helps you with the process of identifying gaps or limitations in your skills and knowledge and encourages you to continue to develop. The second is that, in terms of career progression, being able to demonstrate a record of CPD helps you to show that you have a professional, career-focused approach and that you are continually developing and extending your skills.

> **HOW I BECAME A DATA ANALYST (D)**
>
> I never set out to work with data analytics. I started my career working as a hospital administrator in the NHS, but gravitated towards the systems management side of things. I have always enjoyed working with data; it is very satisfying to see patterns emerge and to know that somewhere, buried in the files and the spreadsheets, is the question which holds the answer to solving a problem. For me, data analysis is about first identifying the questions to ask and then looking for the answers. I've worked in a number of fields, getting formal qualifications along the way and I am now researching in Big Data and Big Data analytics. It is a challenging field because nothing stands still. I constantly have to learn new skills and new approaches. I love it.

Planning your continuous professional development

You will spend a lot of time and effort developing your career. To try and help you make sure that you are identifying the right CPD activities, and that these activities will help you to achieve your career aims, spend some time completing the checklists at the end of this chapter. In the rest of this section, we discuss CPD under three headings: professional activities, technical skills development and soft skills development.

Professional activities

Professional development may involve membership of a professional body and also professional certification. BCS, the Chartered Institute for IT is the recognised professional body for people working in IT in the UK. Membership of BCS gives you access to BCS resources and publications. You will be able to attend meetings and take part in BCS branch activities, such as talks, discussions and visits. You will also be able to join up to five BCS special interest groups. The special interest groups are what the name suggests: the groups are made up of members who meet several times a year to discuss specialist interests. For example, there is a BCS special interest group for data management.

There are five different categories of BCS membership, which match the different stages in your career development. You can join as a Student or Apprentice Member, provided you meet the entry requirements. This will allow you to develop your understanding of the IT industry while you are studying. If you are at the start of your career and do not qualify for student or apprentice membership, you may be able to join as an Associate Member. If you have more experience in the IT industry or have a relevant honours degree, you may be eligible to join as a Professional Member. When you have a track record of professional excellence and contribution to the profession, you can apply to become a Fellow of the British Computer Society. If you do not meet the criteria for membership, but have an interest in the work of BCS, the Chartered Institute for IT, you can apply to become an affiliate member.

Professional membership helps you to network, to share information and experiences with fellow professionals and to develop your understanding of the IT industry in general and your own specialist area in particular. Depending on the field in which you work, you might also join other professional organisations, to help you develop domain knowledge and expert understanding of your field.

Technical skills development

The data analyst role requires good technical skills in a changing data environment. You will need to build on and extend your existing skills and learn new ones.

The audit that you carry out of your skills will allow you to identify the areas that you wish to develop. The skills you need will vary, depending on the area in which you are working and the tools you are using. You might decide to take specialist courses to improve your data analysis skills, such as becoming a specialist in the R programming language, or you might want to take a course in data mining algorithms or statistical analysis. There are a wide range of providers offering training, which ranges from intensive short courses studied in your own time to full-time courses. There are also massively open online courses (MOOCs), which are designed for open access distance learning. MOOCs are usually free and cover a very wide range of subjects.

Participation in specialist groups and forums can also help you to develop your skills. You can post queries and receive replies and as you become more experienced, you can respond to questions from other users and take part in expert discussions.

Professional certification allows you to 'badge' your technical skills and to ensure that your skills remain up to date and relevant in a changing technical environment. Professional certification is provided by most of the major vendors, such as Oracle, Microsoft and Cloudera, and by organisations such as BCS, the Chartered Institute for IT. For example, Microsoft offers a professional programme for data science and BCS offers a professional certificate in data analysis.

You might decide to get additional academic qualifications, for example by taking courses in your own time. Further education colleges, universities and organisations such as the Open University offer a range of courses, many of which can be studied by distance learning.

Before you make a decision about your training needs, you will need to do some research. If you decide that what you need is formal certification, check out the cost of this, what the course will cover and whether the certificate that is awarded is recognised in the workplace. Formal qualifications will have industry and/or government approval. If you decide that you do not need formal certification but want to extend your skills, then make sure that the training course you choose will meet your needs. Suppose, for example, that you want to extend your skills to include expertise with the R programming language: identify what you want to learn about R, check out the course specification, have a look at online reviews to see what other people have said about the different courses and ask around. Sometimes you can do a trial lesson, which will let you check that the course is pitched at the level you need. Many of the online skill courses are free, but some are on a paid-for basis, so always check the small print.

Soft skills development

Chapter 2 discussed the contribution that soft skills can make to the role of the data analyst. CPD for the data analyst is not just about developing technical skills; it also covers the development of soft skills.

Soft skills development is often done in the workplace. Larger companies sometimes run workshops on things such as how to develop team working or communication skills. Smaller companies may not provide this training, or you may wish to organise your own training. Check out what industry and professional training bodies can offer. For example, BCS provides resources and workshops on career development.

Sometimes it is easier to do an audit of technical skills than an audit of softer skills, but as Chapter 2 showed, both sets of skills are needed to succeed as a data analyst. The checklists at the end of the chapter will help you to assess your soft skills.

> A data analyst should be able to understand and articulate the impact of data on their organisation. They should be proficient with data management processes and tooling required to ensure that the data an organisation relies on to make decisions is complete, accurate and fit for purpose.
> (Vicki Leigh-MacKenzie, Data Governance Expert, Nordea)

CAREER PROGRESSION: WHAT NEXT AS A DATA ANALYST?

Once you have become established as a data analyst you might choose to stay in that field and aim to progress eventually to a role such as chief analytical officer or chief data scientist. Alternatively, you might choose to move into a different role, using your analytical skills to enter a field such as business analysis or data management.

Some data analysts follow a very clear career path, moving from junior data analyst, to data analyst, to senior data analyst and then perhaps a role equivalent to chief data analyst. However, as the 'How I become a data analyst' stories in this chapter show, other data analysts often follow different career paths with a variety of routes to becoming a data analyst and progression in the career.

A useful approach is to think about what you want to achieve and when you want to achieve it by so that you can set your own career goals. If you have decided that the data analyst role is for you, then you need to think about how to develop your career. Consider these questions:

- What kind of data analyst do you want to be?
- Where do you see yourself in 5 years' time?
- Where do you see yourself in 10 years' time?
- What do you want to achieve by the end of your career?

CAREER PLANNING

This section will help you to identify the skills and qualifications you will need to become a data analyst and achieve your career goals.

Becoming a data analyst

Now that you have read through this book on the role of the data analyst, you might need to ask yourself some questions. These are covered in this section.

Is this role for me?
A data analyst might work in several arenas. Which part of the data analyst role most appeals to you?

If you have decided that you want to become a data analyst, you need to ask yourself: what qualifications and skills do I already have and what qualifications and skills will I need to develop to make a career in this field?

The best way to answer these questions is carry out a personal audit of your qualifications, skills and aptitudes. By aptitudes, we mean: what do you like and what do you see yourself as being good at? Take the time to think about what you enjoy. If you don't like working with data, for example, you probably shouldn't become a data analyst.

We've provided checklists in Tables 5.1–5.4 to help you carry out your own personal audit; you can use these as they are, or adapt them to provide the basis for your own checklist. We've completed some sections in italics as examples to show you how they work.

These checklists are designed to help you identify your qualifications, skills and aptitudes and also to identify any gaps and areas for future development. When you have completed them, you should have a picture of where you are, what professional development work you need to undertake and which aspects of the data analysis role interest you.

Be realistic, but don't sell yourself short. You need to acknowledge your strengths and the knowledge and experience you already have as well as the areas where you need to develop your skills.

Table 5.1 What qualifications do you have or are about to achieve?

Name of qualification	Date achieved/ about to achieve	How will this help me in the data analyst role?	Do I want to take this further? How can I do this?
For example: BCS Level 4 Certificate in Data Analysis Tools			
For example: BSc in computer science			
List all your qualifications, particularly anything which is relevant to the data analyst role			
List any qualifications that you do not have but would like to achieve			

Table 5.2 What experience do you have that might be relevant to a data analyst career?

List any experience you have that is relevant to the data analyst role	What is my evidence for this?	How will this help me in the data analyst role?	Is there anything I need to do to take this further? How can I do this?
For example: experience with data integration			
For example: experience of communicating with clients			
For example: experience of project management			
Your experience does not have to be computing based; it may be in a field completely unrelated to data analytics, but shows your ability to analyse and interpret data			
List any experience that you do not have, but would like to acquire			

CAREER PROGRESSION OPPORTUNITIES

Table 5.3 What technical skills do you have that might be relevant to the data analyst role?

Technical skill	What evidence do I have that I possess this skill?	How would this skill be relevant to the role of the data analyst?	Do I want to take this further? How can I do this?
For example: use of analytical functions in Excel			
For example: experience with the R programming language			
List any other technical skills that you have			
List any other technical skills that you do not have but would like to acquire			

What personal skills and abilities do you have? Which areas do you feel you need to develop further? These questions are based on the discussion in Chapter 2. If you are not sure what something means, please refer back to Chapter 2.

Table 5.4 What personal skills and abilities do you have?

Skills and abilities	How do I rate myself at this?	What evidence do I have for the rating I have given myself?	Do I want to develop my skills/abilities in this area? How can I do this?
Analytical and problem-solving skills			
How do I rate my analytical skills?			
How do I rate my problem-solving skills?			
Ethics and integrity			
How well do I deal with mistakes?			
How well do I understand the need for governance?			
How well do I understand the data analyst's responsibilities to the stakeholder and other interested parties?			

(Continued)

Table 5.4 (Continued)

Skills and abilities	How do I rate myself at this?	What evidence do I have for the rating I have given myself?	Do I want to develop my skills/abilities in this area? How can I do this?
Communication and working with others			
How well do I communicate with colleagues?			
How well do I communicate with people who don't have my technical background?			
Do I communicate milestones and deadlines effectively?			
Am I good at communicating with the right people?			
Do I present and share information effectively?			
Can I explain my ideas clearly and concisely?			

(Continued)

Table 5.4 (Continued)

Skills and abilities	How do I rate myself at this?	What evidence do I have for the rating I have given myself?	Do I want to develop my skills/abilities in this area? How can I do this?

Team working and team management skills

Do I work well as a member of a team?

How do I handle conflict and conflict resolution?

How well do I perform in a team leader role?

Effective management

Am I good at setting and keeping to deadlines?

How good am I at managing my time effectively?

How good am I at working on my own initiative?

Do I set priorities?

(Continued)

Table 5.4 (Continued)

Skills and abilities	How do I rate myself at this?	What evidence do I have for the rating I have given myself?	Do I want to develop my skills/abilities in this area? How can I do this?
How good are my decision-making skills?			
Dealing with new challenges			
Am I comfortable with new challenges?			
Do I have the personal motivation to keep up to date in a changing data environment?			
Other areas to consider			
What additional personal skills or abilities do I have that might be relevant to the data analyst role?			

(Continued)

Table 5.4 (Continued)

Skills and abilities	How do I rate myself at this?	What evidence do I have for the rating I have given myself?	Do I want to develop my skills/abilities in this area? How can I do this?
What additional personal skills and abilities are there that I would like to extend or develop?			
Are there any limitations or weaknesses which might hold me back?			

Taking this further

Now that you have completed the checklists, you should have a good idea of your strengths and weaknesses, so try completing a SWOT analysis. SWOT stands for strengths (the things you know you are good at), weaknesses (limitations or challenges), opportunities (what opportunities do you see for yourself?) and threats (what things might hold you back or prevent you from succeeding?). Use the diagram in Figure 5.1 to help you to identify your strengths, your weaknesses, the opportunities that are available to you and the things that might hold you back on your journey to becoming a data analyst.

Figure 5.1 SWOT analysis

Strengths

Looking at the checklist you have just completed, what do you feel confident about? What have you identified that will help you to become a data analyst?

Weaknesses

What gaps have you identified? Which areas do you need to work on? Are there any weaknesses that might prevent you from achieving your goal of becoming a data analyst?

Opportunities

What opportunities do you have to move into a data analyst role? What career steps do you need to take?

Threats

What are the things that might hold you back? This is usually linked to any gaps you have identified. Do you need more qualifications and skills? Do you need more experience? Do you need a different work environment?

SUMMARY

In this chapter we have looked at career paths and opportunities for data analysts and at ways in which you can develop your career and gain the skills you need to succeed. You can use the checklists provided in this chapter to carry out an audit of your qualifications, skills and experience and to help you set your career goals. Good luck in your career journey, but be prepared to be flexible about your career plans. As the case studies we have included in this chapter show, things don't always go to plan; sometimes they work out much better than expected.

6 A DAY IN THE LIFE OF A DATA ANALYST

Being a good data analyst is not just about producing beautiful reports and/or dashboards, but also being able to bring out insights from the data and communicate those insights in a plain and logical way to those who need them, to help them make informed decisions. The profession offers great rewards but, as one colleague of this author put it, 'it is very lucrative, but you must muscle your way into it'. For data analysts, there are no idle moments; you are either working or you are learning, or both.

As mentioned in Chapter 5, job opportunities for data analysts can come with different titles, depending on the organisation and the level of responsibility. Consequently, you may see people in the profession bearing different titles such as data analyst, performance analyst, insight analyst, information analyst or business intelligence analyst. They are probably all doing largely the same thing: analysing data and extracting insights to help decision-makers make informed decisions. Knowing that decision-makers depend on you to make the right decisions is quite motivating on its own, but one other great motivator is that you are also being rewarded handsomely by new opportunities that roll out every day. As people move jobs here and there, you can move up the ladder faster than in many other professions.

In this chapter we describe a typical day in the life of a data analyst and offer some tips to guide you as you develop in the role.

A TYPICAL DAY IN THE LIFE OF A DATA ANALYST

6.30 a.m.: It's morning ... again! I'm so used to waking up at this time that I do not need an alarm. I get out of bed and try immediately to make it – I may not do so if I move away from the bedside and it's a small win that puts me in the mindset to get things done at the right time.

I don't have to get out of bed this early every morning, but I enjoy taking a long bus ride to work rather than taking the underground trains.

8.30 a.m.: I have arrived in the office and get a cup of coffee while my computer boots up. The first thing I do on my computer is to update my 'to-do' list. I start by marking the completed tasks and this updates the percentage of tasks completed.

The next thing is to go through my email. Most of my requests or tasks come through email, and it helps me to add or remove items from my 'to-do' list.

These tasks can come thick and fast because I work with policy colleagues in a mental health team, where we have about eight different major programmes running at the same time. Everyone wants their data and/or tools developed first, so there is lots of prioritisation and capacity management involved every morning.

In addition to major projects, I also receive some ad hoc requests and regular reports to work on.

> For ad hoc requests, I keep a log of all of them, then categorise them. This allows me to design and build a report for each category. The reports can be easily updated as data becomes available. This way, you have the answer sometimes before the questions come, and

DATA ANALYST

> you can even train the requesters how to directly use the report to help themselves.
>
> With regard to regular reports (weekly or monthly), I usually automate the process using a tool such as Visual Basic, which saves a lot of time.

After I have prioritised my 'to-do' list, my choice of project for the day is dashboard design, construction and maintenance.[1]

9.00 a.m.: I dial in to a half hour meeting comprising other analyst teams – we refer to this team of colleagues as the Matrix Group. We have offices in six locations all over England and groups of analysts working on different projects in different departments. This is a cross-departmental meeting, an opportunity to hear what everyone's working on and keep in the loop to avoid duplication of work in the organisation.

I think of myself as a bridge between different teams and departments. I need these cross-departmental connections to succeed in my work. I always keep an open professional relationship with the departments and teams I work with; I may end up needing their help for an approaching deadline at short notice.

> In my previous role I was in the Strategy and Policy Team, which is part of a large directorate. I was the only data analyst in the team, so I worked with six other teams

---

[1] My main responsibility as an analyst in this team is building and maintaining internal and external reporting dashboards to provide the policy leads with relevant data and insight to help them in their decision-making processes, and in holding to account the external stakeholders with performance issues.

A DAY IN THE LIFE OF A DATA ANALYST

within three different departments in directorate: Finance, Project Management Office and Communications. My work sometimes extended to external organisations and third-party suppliers. You can only imagine the number of people this involved and the need to be a people person. Some people think being an analyst is just sitting at your desk and crunching all the data given to you. The truth about this role is that all the information you will need for your work is never in one place. Some of the data you need may belong to different departments or even different organisations, and you will not have direct access to such databases. You will, sometimes, have to rely on other analysts to extract the data sets you need to do your job.

What I also try to do often is to find time to go and observe other departments work. I realised that sitting with people in other departments to observe them helps me to understand an organisation better and how it works. How causes and effects are generated and how the business rules are arrived at. The more I get out there to talk to people in other departments, the better I am at deriving insights during analysis.

Many analysts I have met worry that they are not the sort of person that makes friends easily. Well, I wasn't when I started, but I learnt quickly – we all learn and grow into it as time passes by. There are lots of training courses that help too.

After the Matrix meeting, I go straight to the requester/project lead of the task I have selected to start today. We begin the initial requirement gathering to structure the business problem, and discuss and agree on realistic delivery dates for the task.

I find having such meetings early on in the morning helps me to order my thoughts, allowing me to propose likely answers to the questions that stakeholders are trying to ask. These likely answers help me to form ideas of which data to look for to carry out the work.

Generally, the business problems or requests I receive are ill defined and poorly structured. This is mainly because most requesters or project leads often barely know what they want in a dashboard or report. This element of requirement gathering, to understand what they actually want, means that I consider every task as a project. And every project/request is very different, so my initial preparations and research always differs. If the requester does not know what they want at the beginning, which is the case most of the time, they may at least know the KPIs they want to measure. To guide our initial meeting, I always prepare a few questions beforehand, such as:

- Who is the dashboard or report for?
- Is it for different people (managers, finance team, clinicians, marketers, etc.)?
- Are their requirements different?
- Does this change the content of the dashboard or report?
- Who is going to be involved in the project once the scope is agreed?
- What are those groups of people's views about what to include?
- Can you or I engage them in the next stage?
- What would make this dashboard or report innovative and better compared to others?

10.00 a.m.: I start to work on the dashboard design and development based on my discussion with the requester. I like to use Microsoft PowerPoint to design the possible end view of the dashboard, fully labelled and ready for my next meeting with the requester or customer. I find it very useful to engage them every step of the way; that way, I avoid wasting a lot of time and resources developing what they don't want.

The next step is to start gathering the data for cleansing, mining and validation. The amount of time this will take largely depends on the availability, location, accessibility and quality of the data.

As luck would have it, the data I need for my work today is available, close by and of good quality. Some days are not this easy and data gathering takes a lot of time – a day or two, or even more depending on what I am facing at the time.

Individuals may cause some of the issues with data gathering while trying to guard their departmental information. These can be people that are slow to adapt to the change that data is bringing. They find it hard to run with the fact that data is driving everything in this day and age. There are some others that just like to say no, hence consciously or unconsciously blocking or delaying my work.

The potential savings, in terms of time and cost, from data analysis work are very important, which means that things I work on really need to be quick and agile. Thus, if I try to win people over to play along without success, my personal approach is to go to someone higher.

This depends largely on the size and structure of the organisation. When I work in a big team and have a line management structure, it is not within my remit to make these decisions. But whenever I have the autonomy to move around and decide which project to work on, I usually use this approach and move up the hierarchy to get things done if necessary.

Whatever may be the case, I always inform the customers of the current status of their requests to enable them to manage their own expectation and goal setting. It is important to note that data analysis projects are not regular types of project where everything is specified and defined. Even in regular project settings, I have found that things do change from the initial plan – issues arise, so I tend to keep comprehensive issue logs and risk registers. I take into account all the data preparation and data cleaning I have to do, bearing in mind that I can only prepare and clean data after gathering it and, more often than not, the data comes from another department or third-party organisation, which I have no control over.

I also consider the time I use to interview people, who I need to interview, and whether it needs to be more than once. There is a lot of research that goes into this type of work, especially if it's a completely new development and design project. Up to 75 per cent of my work goes into data prepping and cleaning, and, again, that is only when I have all the data – I cannot overemphasise this because it can get tricky. Then I can start driving insight, building models and so on. Safe to say that a lot of major data analysis projects I have worked on are not usually quick fixes.

I always make it clear to the requester what timeframe I anticipate being able to deliver within. This I do by giving myself ample time to plan before agreeing to any deadline, especially for new projects. It is better to under promise and over deliver. I also inform them ahead of time if I think an agreed deadline can no longer be met, and discuss the new deadline as early as possible so that they can adjust their own calendar or commitment.

I make sure that expectations are clear, and I avoid taking on more projects until I deliver the main project at hand.

1.00 p.m.: Lunchtime! I have a one-hour break, so I use half of it to eat, then use the remaining half to take a walk to stretch my legs, socialise and look away from the computer screen. Data analysis is sweet and fulfilling, but if I don't have a break from staring at the screen, I may end up calling my son 'Excel' when I get home!

When I'm back from my walk, I still have few minutes of my lunch break left, so I socialise with colleagues before returning to work. I use this to promote my data culture campaign advocacy skills by speaking to whoever cares to listen about the importance of data and how it can make their job easier. I always endeavour to do everything possible to win people over to the 'data side', and create some level of data culture with every task and project I embark on.

We live in a time and age when everything we do accumulates data. Data is really taking over, from our wearable gadgets, to social media footprints and sensors that use data to feed into businesses to help decision-making. Data has changed the way things are done, not just in running businesses but also in politics and our personal life.

Everybody is now expected to know how to use a smartphone. This was not the case 10 years ago. It is safe to say that 10 years from now, everyone in a workplace will be expected to have some level of data literacy. As a data analyst, whenever I have the opportunity to talk to different people at different levels of my organisation, I always have at the back of my mind the intent of creating a data culture. I utilise every opportunity I have to work with people to express some form of data advocacy.

How do I do that? I feel it is my duty to show people how decisions based on data can make their work easier and even more interesting and satisfying. I try to help them to understand that apart from making their jobs easier, the world is moving towards data analysis and everything will be driven by it. Even if it is not compulsory to work with data now it will be in the near future, so the earlier they start becoming data friendly the better for them.

The people I win over at an early stage of my data advocacy have helped me in creating the data culture. They open up conversations on my behalf and it becomes easier to approach other people in the organisation.

Some people may think that creating such a culture is for the managers; I can assure you that anybody can embark on the task.

2.00 p.m.: I finalise the dashboard design, with the data almost ready, and I send an invite to the requester for another meeting to look at the initial design and discuss any data or other issues that have arisen during the data preparation stage. I always do initial research before embarking on any project; however, the actual situation of things only emerge when I have started the job proper.

I assemble all my initial findings and work to present a better view of the project to the requester and head to this second meeting. This helps me to clarify and validate the work and pre-existing information with the requester. It is also a good time to look at the delivery date to make sure we're on the same page. But it was a successful morning, as the data was available and of good quality, so the meeting goes smoothly and I go back to the actual work quickly.

Having said that, common practice is that people will just come to me and ask me for an insight from a data set without any explanation or even the slightest idea of what they are looking for. In such cases, second meetings like this will take much more time and possibly end with a complete scope change. To bring that type of situation under control, I always make it clear from the start that I cannot just start working on a data set without proper discussion.

Thus, while developing the data culture at work, I try to set expectations. I make it clear how my colleagues should put across their requests for capacity management and priority setting. There must be an initial meeting to elicit what is needed or the problem the requestor is facing. I make it a point of duty to remind them that every task or project should come to me as a business-specific problem. I work with them to pinpoint what the issues are and what they want to solve. Instead of dumping data on me and asking for insight, they should be able to come up with questions such as:

- Do we receive more complaints over weekend shifts than weekdays?
- Are products not on time on Tuesdays?
- What is the cause of absenteeism on Mondays?

With those types of questions, I have an idea of what they are trying to look for. Those will actually help me to identify the right data set. Take, for instance, the question of receiving complaints over weekends; I may start with segmenting the callers by age, educational background or ethnicity. That way I will have a direction of travel for the analysis. The whole process of engaging in different analysis and deriving insights makes up the project journey. Sometimes I come up with insights that are irrelevant to the task at hand, but could be useful in solving other problems.

4.15 p.m.: I remember that I have not looked at my email since this morning, because I always close it down after each check as the alert at the bottom of my screen is a distraction. So, I take a quick look and there are even more urgent requests sent about an hour ago. I was really keen to deliver the dashboard today – at least the first draft – but there is a more pressing request from one of the directors. They have a meeting first thing in the morning with people in the government and they have requested a piece of work ready before 8 a.m. the next day. Luckily, I have some of the output in another report I produced previously, so it makes the design and delivery of the request somewhat easier and quicker.

As I developed in the profession, emails like this became common; everyone comes to me for any issue they have. People in the organisation talk more about me and how I add value to the organisation – how I am the go-to person for solving difficult bottlenecks. I always end up with too many requests that I have no chance of handling on my own. That is when the word 'no' becomes very handy. Saying no in the workplace can be difficult because everyone is working for the same goal using different approaches.

Bearing in mind that all projects are important (at least, someone in the organisation thinks they are), I have learnt the best way to say 'no' in order not to compromise the good working relationships I've developed over time. Now, some projects may be interesting and others not so interesting, but as a data analyst, what guides my decision on which project is the priority is the business value it generates. I assess every project based on what the outcome will mean to the business – how much value the end product will add. I consider this for all the available options before selection. I never choose a project on the mere fact that it is most interesting to me personally or that the requester is my friend.

These decisions are not solely up to me much of the time. I may need to discuss them with my line manager, but I am always ready to put my views across. Consequently, I make sure I have developed criteria to back up my argument before going into such meetings.

I recently persuaded senior management in my organisation to approve the use of a proforma system for job requests. This is just a simple system where the requester will have to complete a proforma for every request. Everyone in the organisation is well aware that the request can come back as approved with a delivery date, be postponed or be redirected to another team. This has made it a lot easier to manage workload and has become so popular that they have rolled it out to the wider organisation. Sometimes I really don't have to say the 'no' face to face.

However, this system does not stop me from scheduling 10–20 minutes to explain to the declined project requesters what other project I am working on and why I picked that over theirs. This is why it is important to have those job selection criteria at hand. Imagine if your decision is based on your personal interest, you will be making a lot of enemies in the organisation or even risk putting your job in jeopardy. Everyone usually understands a business value-driven decision.

I personally measure value-to-business based on monetary terms, efficiency or customer satisfaction – although it could be a million things, depending on the organisation. This line of thinking also helps me when explaining why I prioritise one project over another to the requestors. I believe it helps them to easily see that my decision is purely business, and nothing personal.

> The best way to say no is by starting with an explanation of how I come up with the decision of not taking up their project. So, never say 'yes' outright when a request is proposed. Always give yourself a little time to assess and evaluate each project.

Sometimes I prepare guidance notes to help the requester achieve their goal on their own for those projects I turn down. I may discover that the task they intend to carry out has been done in the past somewhere in the organisation. It saves them time, helping them to avoid reinventing the wheel. And it also helps me build good relationships and learn more about every part of the business and how things work – moving me closer and closer to creating that data culture.

> I have done a project on patient access rate in NHS service providers. I was working for a central organisation that monitors such service providers. The problem was that the project requester believed that patient referral rate had a direct effect on the access rate. The task was to identify those service providers with lower referral rates. This allowed the support team from my organisation to develop a plan that helped them to increase referral rates. My initial analysis showed that a decrease in attrition rate would increase access rate. Further analysis and optimisation showed that reducing waiting time would decrease attrition, which would in turn increase access rate, even at the current referral rate. My recommendation made it easier to achieve the target access rate much more easily and cheaply for the organisations. After the project, I went back to the requester and the teams and offered to do a presentation of my work and how I arrived at my result and recommendation. They were very happy and grateful that I had made the gesture. They gained a better understanding of how the data was used to change the course of action more cheaply and quickly to reach the desired goal.

A DAY IN THE LIFE OF A DATA ANALYST

5.30 p.m.: I have just rounded off the urgent request, printed hardcopies and sent the softcopy to the director's secretary via email. I always provide softcopies in case the requestors want to make changes; and if I'm not in the office, another analyst could help.

I then decide to check my email again before leaving – stupid move, I must confess. But it ended up becoming a blessing in disguise as I was able to reply to three different requests, informing them that I am unable to pick up their task because tomorrow I plan to finish the dashboard I started this morning.

As well as the dashboard, I have a presentation to develop first thing tomorrow morning and present to the director in a meeting. I quickly shutdown and run for my bus.

7.15 p.m.: I've been home for around 10 minutes, and am having my dinner. I usually go for a one-hour gym session on days like this, but I got home a bit later than usual due to the last minute requests. I have a bath and watch a movie.

I find that relaxing with a movie or gym before preparing a presentation allows me to come down to a non-technical level and help the audience (mostly non-technical) understand me. In my relaxed mood, I start to visualise the start 'A' and the end 'B' for the presentation I need to prepare tomorrow; presentation, for me, is about taking my audience through that journey from point 'A' to point 'B'. This entails being able to extract the 'so what?' of each analysis. There is the need to communicate recommendations effectively, providing arguments to underpin the case to be made to stakeholders, especially the decision-makers. Not all of the data and information needs to be included in the final presentation.

Presenting to the executives is always daunting, especially for me when I was just starting out. Whenever I step into a boardroom, I know right away that I will have to say something of value. I always prepare and accept the fact that it could be a scary experience, but I always have at the back of my mind that they are just humans. They are people like me, very busy, but still people.

I present to them like I would to every other audience. The only difference is the content of my presentation. Executives are impatient and always interested in the numbers – monetary values.

They are interested in:

- how much the project will make them;
- how much they will save; and
- how much it will cost to achieve.

Whatever I find during my analysis, I always try to quantify it in monetary values when presenting to executives.

But the truth is not always pretty. As a data analyst, I am looking at the facts and figures. Sometimes, I discover very uncomfortable truths that could be challenging to someone in the organisation. Sometimes, my findings will not resonate with the people I will be presenting them to. For instance, my analysis may uncover an inefficiency or performance issue in a popular department. I am always prepared for such awkward situations – it happens all the time as a data analyst, and I am used to it.

One way of getting myself prepared for such eventualities is by preparing my audience as well. I discuss it with them beforehand once my insight starts to show something ugly and unpalatable. This helps to prepare them; I try to let them know that I am mining for the facts and that some facts may not be what they will want to hear. That way, I am not taking them completely unawares when the final report arrives.

Most importantly, I find time to look at my write-up over and over again, adding or removing material as required, then rehearsing with my peers or colleagues if time permits; although I tend not to worry too much about remembering all I need to say or the order I have to say it. What I always have on my mind is how I am going to impress my audience. How I am going to share the knowledge and get them excited. Whenever I am in front of an audience, they can feel the passion for what I want to talk about.

11.00 p.m.: Bedtime! I go to sleep now, feeling ready to start my presentation in the morning.

TOP TIPS FOR DATA ANALYSTS

If you are starting out or already in the analytics profession, here are few top tips for you, to summarise this book:

- Always plan to acquire new knowledge and reinvent yourself during your career. I spend about 5 hours every week on learning and development and keeping up to date with the latest news in my industry. Keep learning and reading; no knowledge is a waste.

- Always speak up and speak out. You are in the business of fact finding – do not be afraid to speak out to state a fact. You are no lesser a human than anyone else in the hierarchy.

- Don't be a data chimp or a one trick pony. In the world of tabular data, it's much more important to know the business rather than advanced algorithms. Get exposure of different functional areas and different industries.

- Never assume that whatever is being done is the most effective approach of doing it. Business as usual is overrated. Always challenge the status quo.
- We all have creative minds, so develop yours to focus more on innovation. You will come out with new ideas rather than doing business as usual.
- Do not waste your time thinking how much effort you have spent on a particular project. You cannot recoup that effort. Instead, consider the opportunity cost, and ask yourself the question: given what I know now, what is the best course of action? Sometimes the best course of action may be to change projects, regardless of how attached you are to the one you are working on.
- One of the biggest gaps in the analytics profession is soft skills, especially communication. Develop great communication skills and watch yourself fly.
- Put yourself up for challenges with your peers. You can achieve a lot by participating in career-related competitions and events.
- When you study and learn, you have insights for others. So, write articles, white papers and blogs on your subject matter.
- As you perfect your data analysis trade, more people will seek you out for help. Be humble – no matter what your experience is, there is always someone better than you.
- You can always use more relationships across every organisation you work with, and beyond. Reach out to people, ask questions about their work and listen intently.
- Finally, get yourself a mentor. Actively seek feedback from your managers, peers and friends alike. Always maintain clear visibility of your strengths, opportunities and weaknesses.

> Data without data analysts is like a sailboat without a sail.
> (Emilie Pons, PhD in mathematics, experienced industry professional)

Have a successful and fruitful career!

REFERENCES

CHAPTER 1

Davenport, T.H. and Patil, D.J. (2012) 'Data scientist: the sexiest job of the 21st century'. *Harvard Business Review*, October Issue. Available from: https://hbr.org/2012/10/data-scientist-the-sexiest-job-of-the-21st-century [13 December 2018].

Laney, Doug (2001) '3D data management: controlling data volume, velocity and variety'. *META Group Res. Note*, 6 (70). Available from: https://blogs.gartner.com/doug-laney/files/2012/01/ad949-3D-Data-Management-Controlling-Data-Volume-Velocity-and-Variety.pdf [13 December 2018].

Sutton, D. (2017) *Cyber Security: A Practitioner's Guide*. Swindon, UK: BCS Learning & Development Ltd.

CHAPTER 3

Bennett, N. and AXELOS (2017) *Managing Successful Projects with PRINCE2*. Norwich, UK: The Stationery Office.

Inmon, W.H. (2005) *Building the Data Warehouse*, 4th edn. Indianapolis, USA: Wiley Publishing inc.

Kimball, R. and Ross, M. (2013) *The Data Warehouse Toolkit: The Definitive Guide to Dimensional Modelling*, 3rd edn. Indianapolis, USA: John Wiley & Sons Inc.

Measey, P., Levy, R., Roberts, B., et al. (2015) *Agile Foundations: Principles, Practices and Frameworks*. Swindon, UK: BCS Learning & Development Ltd.

Trevino, A. (2016) 'Introduction to K-means Clustering'. *Oracle + DataScience.com*, 6 December 2016. Available from: https://www.datascience.com/blog/k-means-clustering [18 January 2016].

CHAPTER 4

Botsman, Rachel (2017a) *Who Can You Trust? How Technology Brought Us Together and Why It Might Drive Us Apart*. New York, USA: Portfolio Penguin.

Botsman, Rachel (2017b) 'Big Data meets Big Brother as China moves to rate its citizens'. *Wired*, 21 October. Available from: www.wired.co.uk/article/chinese-government-social-credit-score-privacy-invasion [13 December 2018].

Mystal, Elie (2008) 'The case for sleep: what happens in Excel after dark'. *Above the Law*, 10 October. Available from: https://abovethelaw.com/2008/10/the-case-for-sleep-what-happens-in-excel-after-dark/ [13 December 2018].

FURTHER READING

CHAPTER 1

Burdett, A., Bowen, D., Butler, D., et al. (2013) *BCS Glossary of Computing*, 14th edn. Swindon, UK: BCS Learning & Development Ltd.

Davenport, T.H., Harris, J.G. and Morison, R. (2010) *Analytics at Work: Smarter Decisions, Better Results*. Boston, USA: Harvard Business Review Press.

CHAPTER 3

Celko, J. (2014) *Joe Celko's SQL for Smarties: Advanced SQL Programming*, 5th edn. Waltham, USA: Morgan Kaufman.

Fandango, A. (2017) *Python Data Analysis*, 2nd edn. Birmingham, UK: Packt Publishing.

Golfarelli, M. and Rizzi, S. (2009) *Data Warehouse Design: Modern Principles and Methodologies*. Bologna, Italy: McGraw-Hill.

Gordon, K. (2017) *Modelling Business Information*. Swindon, UK: BCS Learning & Development Ltd.

Grolemund, G. (2014) *Hands-On Programming with R: Write Your Own Functions and Simulations*. Farnham, UK: O'Reilly Media.

Matthes, E. (2016) *Python Crash Course: A Hands-On, Project-Based Introduction to Programming*. San Francisco, USA: No Starch Press Inc.

FURTHER READING

McGrath, M. (2018) *R for Data Analysis in Easy Steps*. Leamington Spa, UK: In Easy Steps Ltd.

Molinaro, A. (2005) *SQL Cookbook*. Farnham, UK: O'Reilly Media.

Paul, D., Cadle, J., Yeates, D., et al. (2014) *Business Analysis*, 3rd edn. Swindon, UK: BCS Learning & Development Ltd.

Peck, R., Olsen, C. and Devore, J. (2015) *Introduction to Statistics and Data Analysis*, 5th edn. Boston, USA: Cengage Learning.

Ramalho, L. (2015) *Fluent Python*. Farnham, UK: O'Reilly Media.

Taylor, A.G. (2013) *SQL For Dummies*, 8th edn. Hoboken, USA: John Wiley & Sons Inc.

INDEX

accuracy 112, 112n15
adaptability 33–4
advanced query techniques 75
Agile Alliance 87
Agile software 86
Amazon.com 92
analyst B 136
analyst C 140
analyst D 143
analytical thinking 37–8
anonymisation
  aggregation 104
  nulling out/deletion 105
  number/date variance 105
  shuffling 105
  substitution 104
Apache Hadoop system 9, 77
Apple 90
appropriateness 113
articulation 47–8
audience 44–7
AXELOS 86

Basel norms 25
BCS (Chartered Institute for IT)
  Code of Conduct of 18
  membership 144
  resources and workshops 146
  special interest groups 144
  training offers 136
  vision of 16
  website 137
bias
  reporting 62
  sampling 63
  selection 62
Big Data
  analytics 143
  arrival of 129
  career progression 131, 133
  emergence of 1, 6–7
  programming tools 54
  refined techniques 69
Botsman, Rachel 91
British Computer Society 144

budgets 48, 123–4
business
  analysis 78–84, 128–9
  information degrees 139
  intelligence teams (BI) 110
  modellers 129
  understanding organisation/processes 30
business as usual requests (BAU) 38

C# 53
capability 17, 32, 41
career building
  becoming an analyst B 136
  becoming an analyst C 140
  becoming an analyst D 143
  best degree subjects 138–9
  Data Analyst Apprenticeship Scheme 137–8
  degrees in a different subject 140

getting started 135–6

graduate training schemes 141

higher education qualifications 138

usefulness of an MSc 141

career development

continuous professional development (CPD) 142–4

professional activities 144

soft skills 146–7, 174

technical skills 145–6

career planning

experience 150

personal audit 148

personal skills 152–6

qualifications 149

the role of an analyst 148

SWOT analysis 156–7

taking it further 156

technical skills 151

career progression

analyst/scientist 133

analytical officers/chief 133

architects 134

assurance and quality 132

Big Data 131

business analysts 134

business innovator/transformation managers 134

business intelligence 130

changing role of analysts 129

consultants 134

data analytics/data mining 131

engineers 134

example 130–1

introduction 128

logistics managers 135

mixed analytics 132

moving forward 148

operational research 131

paths for analysts 129–30

project managers 134

cause and effect diagram see Fishbone diagram

central processing units (CPUs) 9

Certificate in Data Analysis Tools 137

change management 50, 84–5, 88

Chief Data Officers (CDOs) 110

classification 94–5

cloud solutions 8

Cloudera 145

coding

central repository of 48

VBA 32

writing 32

communication 33, 43–4, 174

computer science

advances in 6

degrees in 139

conflict resolution 38–9

consistency 115–16

continuous professional development (CPD) 129, 142–4

contracts 87, 101, 114

coupling 72–3

courses 42, 48, 69, 88, 130–1, 139, 145–6, 161

credit risk data analysts 25

CRISP-DM 3

cybersecurity experts 35

dashboards 119, 130, 158, 160–2, 160n1, 166–8, 171

data

availability of 28

bias 62–3

breaches 107–9

classification 94–5

cleansing 60, 163–4

community 120–4

culture 165–7, 170

description of 2–3

descriptive analytics 63

encryption 105–6

extraction 59–60

free, open and public 8

governance 109–10

groupings of 56

job descriptions/tasks 22–3, 26–7

key industries 24

loading 62

management expectations of 4–5

181

manipulation of 58
master 57
mining 131, 163, 172–3
other people's 90–1
owners 123
personal 16–17
privacy concerns 13–14
quality of 111–20
reference 58
reformatting of 61
responsibilities of an analyst 29
science 11–12
security 102–9
statistical analysis 62
stewards 122–3
structured 7
transactional 57
transformation 60
unstructured 7
users 121–2
variables 63–7
data analysts
  Apprenticeship Scheme 137–8
  description of 137
  entry requirements 137–8
  helping a career 138
  job titles 158
  life of 159–73
  tips for 173–5
data centric software 31
data modelling 51, 78–84
Data Protection Acts (1984/1998) 91
data science degrees 138

data storage architecture 23
Data Subject Rights 98
databases
  graph 52–3
  NoSQL 52
  object-oriented 53
db4o 53
debugging functionality 55
decision-making 2–4, 22, 41–3, 133
declarative language 73
diagrams
  entity-relationship 79
  Unified Modelling Language 83–4
Diploma in Data Analysis Concepts 137
documenting 125–6

economics degrees 139
employees 51–2
entities 51–2
Entity-relationship diagrams
  conceptual model 79
  logical model 79
  physical model 79
ethics 18, 35
extraction transformation and loading skills (ETL) 31

Facebook 89, 92, 109
feedback 26–8, 45–6, 174
Fishbone diagram 40
floppy disks 34

focus groups 37
formal certification 146
four eyes testing 120

Gantt charts 40
General Data Protection Regulation 2016 (GDPR)
  accuracy 98
  anonymisation 103–5
  data classification 94–5
  data minimisation 98
  explanation 13, 18, 92–3
  integrity and confidentiality 99
  lawful bases 99–102
  personal data 95–7
  pseudonymisation 106
  purpose limitation 98
  sensitive personal data 97–8
  storage limitation 98–9
  summary 127
general linear models 66
Google 92
governance committees 123–4
GraphDB 53
graphical displays 56
graphical processing (GPUs) 9
graphs/figures 47

Hadoop languages 54, 77
health and social care 16

Heraclitus 33
Higher National Certificate (HNC) 137–8
Higher National Diploma (HND) 138
hypothesis-driven approaches 45

IBM Db2 52
ICO website 95, 102
IF statements 70
imperative programming
  iteration 70
  selection 70
  sequencing 70
industry knowledge requirements 24–6
Information Commissioner 19, 92
insight teams 46
integrated development environments (IDEs) 54–5
interactive aggregations 56
Internet of Things (IoT) 6
interpreter/compilers 55
Ishikawa diagram *see* Fishbone diagram
issue logs 164
issue trackers 119–20
IT industry 24, 26

jargon 47
Java language 53–4, 77
Jupyter Notebook 54

KDD 3
KPIs (key performance indicators) 130

Laney, Doug 6
learning
  curves 34
  opportunities 49
  supervised 68
  support vector machines 68
  unsupervised 68
legacy management information teams (MI) 110
legal considerations 12–13
Lehman Brothers 114
lineage mappings 125–6, 125n19
linear regression model 66
listening 36–7
Little Britain (TV show) 15
loops 70
low usage 28

machine learning 10–11, 67
management teams 110
MapReduce programming model 77
mathematics and statistics degrees 139
Matlab language 54, 77
matplotlib 69
Matrix Group 160–1
Measey et al. (2015) 87
mentoring 174
metadata 57
methods 57–69

Microsoft Access 52
Microsoft data science programme 145
Microsoft Excel 69, 77, 114, 119
Microsoft PowerPoint 46, 162
Microsoft SQL Server 52
Microsoft Visio 126
milestones/goals 44
models
  data warehouse 81
  Kimball dimensional 82
  object-oriented 82
  relational 79–81
  star and snowflake schema 82–3
MOOCs (massive open online courses) 145
multiple choice question test (MCQ) 137
MySQL 52

National Vocational Qualification, Level 4 (NVQ) 137
natural language processing 11
negotiation skills 38
Neo4j 53
Net promoter scores (NPS) 37, 37n4
NHS 143, 170
normalisation 80–1
NoSQL databases 18
NS&I 104

object-oriented programming languages 53
ObjectDatabase++ 53

183

ObjectDB 53
Office for National Statistics (ONS) 114
online analytical processing cube tools (OLAP) 61
open access distance learning 145
open-source relational database systems 52
opportunity costs 174
Oracle 145
Oracle RDBMS 52

Pearson coefficient 64–5
PEBCAK 120
personal data
  breaches 99
  description 95–7
  lawful bases for processing 99–102
personal identifiable information (PII) 95
Plotly library 56
predictive analytics 65–7
Premium Bonds 104
presentation 33, 46
PRINCE2 project management method 85–7
prioritisation 41
Privacy and Electronic Communications Regulations (PECR) 92
problem-solving 39
product life cycles 27
proforma systems 169
programming
  declarative 71
  functional 71–2
  imperative 69–70
  languages 32, 69
  modularisation 72–3
project management 84–6
proprietary languages 77–8
provenance 124–7
pseudonymisation 106–7
public interest 18, 101–2
public sector 3
PyCharm 54
Python language 53–4, 69, 76–7

Q&A sessions 48
Qlikview 56
quality
  defining 111–16
  improving 119–20
  measuring 116
  monitoring 116–19
  Six Sigma 111

R 54, 69
  programming language 145
relational database management systems (RDBMS) 17, 53, 73
risk registers 164
root cause analysis 122
Royal Statistical Society 19

sampling 43, 63, 132
SAS language 54, 77
scientific/medical research 131
seaborn 69
security 14–15
SEMMA 3
sensor data 131
sentiment analysis 131
service level agreements (SLAs) 38
SFIA 138
skills
  Advanced Microsoft Excel 32
  functional 30, 49
  key technical 31–2
  soft 31–3, 49
  technical 30–1, 49
Skills Framework for the Information Age (SFIA) 26
Slice Intelligence 90
smartphones 34, 165
social media 131
soft skills 146–7, 174
software code editors 55
software development environments (SDEs) 54–5
supervised learning
  genetic algorithms 68
  neural networks 68
SPSS language 54, 77
Spyder IDE 54
SQL SELECT statement 73–6
SQL (Structured Query Language) 8, 17, 53, 71, 73, 77
stakeholders 33, 36–42, 44–6, 48, 123, 161–2
statistical analysis techniques 10
statistical software 32
storage
  distributed 7–8
  limitation 98–9

Structured Query Language (SQL) 8, 17, 53, 71, 73
subject matter experts (SMEs) 29, 39, 48
SWOT analysis 156–7

Tableau 56
task management 33, 40
team profiles 48–9
technical skills 145–6
template web pages 69
testing
　integration 78
　regression 78
　unit 77–8
text mining 131
three-layer architecture
　detailed 81
　mart 81–2
　staging 81
time management 40–1

time-boxing 87
timeliness 113
tools
　databases 50
　introduction 50
　programming 54–6
　relational databases 51–2

Uber 90
Unified Modelling Language (UML) 83
uniqueness 114–15
United Kingdom
　data protection regulations in 13
　data.gov.uk initiative 4
　leading the with large data sets 19
unroll.me 90

validation 115, 163
variables
　correlation 64
　dependent 66

　description 63
　independent 66
　interpolation/extrapolation 66–7
　meaning 10
　regression analysis 65–6
　significance 65
VBA 77
Visual Basic tool 160
visualisation 11, 55–6, 68–9
visualisation tools 29–30
voice of customers (VOC) 37, 37n5

warehousing 23, 58–9, 61, 125, 131
Wetherspoons 100
Wired magazine 91
workshops 48

Y2K issue 26, 26n3